D1627318

Th
late
of t

D

VENUS & ADONIS
THE RAPE OF LUCRECE
THE PHŒNIX & TURTLE

by William Shakespeare

London: J. M. DENT & SONS LTD.
New York: E. P. DUTTON & CO. INC.

Editor's General Note

The Text. The editor has kept before him the aim of presenting to the modern reader the nearest possible approximation to what Shakespeare actually wrote. The text is therefore conservative, and is based on the earliest reliable printed text. But to avoid distraction (*a*) the spelling is modernised, and (*b*) a limited number of universally accepted emendations is admitted without comment. Where a Quarto text exists as well as the First Folio the passages which occur only in the Quarto are enclosed in square brackets [ ] and those which occur only in the Folio in brace brackets { }.

Scene Division. The rapid continuity of the Elizabethan curtainless production is lost by the 'traditional' scene divisions. Where there is an essential difference of place these scene divisions are retained. Where on the other hand the change of place is insignificant the scene division is indicated only by a space on the page. For ease of reference, however, the 'traditional' division is retained at the head of the page and in line numbering.

Notes. Passages on which there are notes are indicated by a † in the margin.

Punctuation adheres more closely than has been usual to the 'Elizabethan' punctuation of the early texts. It is often therefore more indicative of the way in which the lines were to be delivered than of their syntactical construction.

Glossaries are arranged on a somewhat novel principle, not alphabetically, but in the order in which the words or phrases occur. The editor is much indebted to Mr J. N. Bryson for his collaboration in the preparation of the glossaries.

Preface

VENUS AND ADONIS

The Text. The poem was first published in 1593 with the following title-page: VENVS / AND ADONIS / *Vilia miretur vulgus : mihi flauus Apollo / Pocula Castalia plena ministret aqua.* / LONDON / Imprinted by Richard Field, and are to be sold at / the signe of the white Greyhound in / Paules Church-yard. / 1593.

The text, apart from some odd punctuation, is excellently printed, and, as the numerous succeeding Quartos have no independent authority, the text which follows is that of Q 1 with the spelling, and to some small extent the punctuation, regularised.

Date of Composition. The only certainty we have is that the poem must have been written before the entry in the Stationers' Registers of April 1593. If we take the remark in the dedication about ' the first heire of my inuention ' in its obvious sense, then, whatever views we hold about *Henry VI*, we must put *Venus and Adonis* at any rate earlier than *Richard III* and *The Comedy of Errors*, and the dating of the poem depends on the dating of the plays.

Source. The story was common enough in various shapes, but the direct source was presumably Ovid's *Metamorphoses* (whether in the original or in Golding's translation of 1567) with the story of Venus and Adonis in the tenth book, and that of Salmacis and Hermaphroditus in the fourth.

For the verse form Shakespeare perhaps turned to Lodge's *Glaucus and Scilla.*

THE RAPE OF LUCRECE

The Text. The poem was first published in Quarto in 1594, with the following title-page : LUCRECE. / LONDON. / Printed by Richard Field, for Iohn Harrison, and are / to be sold at the signe of the white Greyhound / in Paules Church yard. 1594. It was reprinted seven times by 1655. The fifth quarto (1616) shows unmistakable signs of a process of editorial revision, but there is no evidence, and not much probability, that the revision was by Shakespeare, and the text here given is that of 1594. This text is well printed, and requires almost no emendation, except in the punctuation, which is somewhat erratic. Some of the most remarkable variants of Q 5 are recorded in the notes.

(Q 1 was evidently corrected as the sheets were being printed off, since one of the copies in the Bodleian Library has five readings which are 'corrected' in all the other nine extant copies; both copies in the Bodleian have one reading which is corrected in the remaining eight, and three copies concur in two pretty obvious misprints against the other seven. Since the activities of the press-corrector seem usually to have been conducted by the light of his intelligence rather than by reference to the MS., we have in these cases to choose between the compositor and the corrector. I usually prefer the compositor.)

Date of Composition. The poem was entered in the Stationers' Registers in May of 1594. *Venus and Adonis* was entered in April of the preceding year. We may reasonably assign the composition of *Lucrece* to 1593-94.

Sources. The story of Lucrece was a favourite one, and often handled. If we are determined to find specific sources the second book of Ovid's *Fasti*, the second novel of Painter's *Palace of Pleasure*, Chaucer's *Legende of Good Women*, and perhaps (verbally) Daniel's *Complaint of Rosamond* should content us.

The Verse. The stanza form of *Lucrece* is the famous *Rime Royal*, the stanza of *Troilus and Criseyde*, of *The Kingis Quair*, of Sackville's *Induction* and Spenser's *Ruines of Time*. James VI of Scotland in his *Reulis and Cautelis of Scottis Poesie* advises the use of this kind of verse, ' callit *Troilus verse*, for tragicall materis, complaintis, or testamentis.'

Criticism.

Hazlitt.—The two poems of *Venus and Adonis* and of *Tarquin and Lucrece* appear to us like a couple of ice-houses. They are about as hard, as glittering and as cold. The author seems all the time to be thinking of his verses, and not of his subject,—not of what his characters would feel, but of what he shall say; and as it must happen in all such cases, he always puts into their mouths those things which they would be the last to think of, and which it shews the greatest ingenuity in him to find out. The whole is laboured, up-hill work. The poet is perpetually singling out the difficulties of the art to make an exhibition of his strength and skill in wrestling with them. He is making perpetual trials of them as if his mastery over them were doubted. The images, which are often striking, are generally applied to things which they are the least like : so that they do not blend with the poem, but seem stuck upon it, like splendid patchwork, or remain quite distinct from it, like detached substances, painted and varnished over. A beautiful thought is sure to be lost in an endless commentary upon it. The speakers are like persons who have both leisure and inclination to make riddles on their own situation, and to twist and turn every object or incident into acrostics and anagrams. Every thing is spun into an allegory; and a digression is always preferred to the main story. Sentiment is built up upon plays of words; the hero or heroine feels, not from the impulse of passion, but from the force of dialectics. There is besides a strange attempt to substitute the language of painting for that of poetry, to make us *see* their feelings in the faces of the persons; and again, consistently with this, in the description of the picture in *Tarquin and Lucrece*, those circumstances are chiefly insisted on, which it would be impossible to convey except by words.

Coleridge.—The Venus and Adonis did not perhaps allow the display of the deeper passions. But the story of Lucretia seems to favour, and even demand, their intensest workings. And yet we find in Shakespeare's management of the tale neither pathos nor any other dramatic quality. There is the same minute and faithful imagery as in the former poem, in the same vivid colours, inspirited by the same impetuous vigour of thought, and diverging and contracting with the same activity of the assimilative and of the modifying faculties; and with a yet larger display, and a wider range of knowledge and reflection; and lastly, with the same perfect dominion, often domination, over the whole world of language. What, then, shall we say? even this, that Shakespeare, no mere child of nature, no automaton of genius; no passive vehicle of inspiration possessed by the spirit, not possessing it; first studied patiently, meditated deeply, understood minutely, till knowledge, become habitual and intuitive, wedded itself to his habitual feelings, and at length gave birth to that stupendous power, by which he stands alone, with no equal or second in his own class ; to that power which seated him on one of the two glory-smitten summits of the poetic mountain, with Milton as his compeer not rival. . . . All things and modes of action shape themselves anew in the being of Milton ; while Shakespeare becomes all things, yet for ever remaining himself. O what great men hast thou produced, England ! my country ! Truly, indeed,

> *Must we be free or die, who speak the tongue,*
> *Which Shakespeare spake ; the faith and morals hold,*
> *Which Milton held ; in every thing we are sprung*
> *Of earth's first blood, have titles manifold.*

THE PHŒNIX AND TURTLE

At the end of *Love's Martyr*, a poem by one Robert Chester, published in 1601, was appended a section thus described :—Hereafter Follow Diuerse Poeticall Essaies on the former Subject ; viz.: the Turtle and Phœnix. Done by the best and chiefest of our moderne writers, with their names subscribed to their particular workes. Amongst these (which include poems by Jonson, Chapman, and Marston) are some verses, with no title, to which Shakespeare's name is appended.

Note.—*The Passionate Pilgrim* and *A Lover's Complaint* are omitted from this edition. The Shakespearean authorship of the latter and of all but five pieces of the former is a good deal worse than dubious. Of the five pieces in *The Passionate Pilgrim* i. and ii. are versions of Sonnets cxxxviii. and cxliv., and iii., v., and xvii. are 'poetic missives' from *Love's Labour's Lost*.   There are verbal variants, notably in i.; and if one could be sure that the versions in *The Passionate Pilgrim* were early drafts they would be worth giving.   But in fact we cannot be sure that the versions were the result of anything but faulty memorisation or careless copying.

line

516 WITH THY LIFE'S DECAY, along with yourself
530 SIMPLE, drug
COMPACTED, included
534 TENDER, accept
537 SLAVISH WIPE, slave's brand
540 COCKATRICE, a serpent reputed to kill with glance of eye (basilisk)
543 GRIPE, gryphon
553 WINKS, shuts his eyes
565 PERIOD, full-stop
FROM, out of
HIS, its
569 GENTRY, 'gentlehood'
576 PRETENDED, proposed
581 UNSEASONABLE, out of season
629 PATTERN'D, given an example
637 ASKANCE, turn aside
643 EYNE, eyes
646 LET, hindrance
695 TENDER, sensitive
696 BALK, miss
701 CONCEIT, conception
703 RECEIPT, what he has taken in
707 JADE, poor horse
724 IN, into
743 CONVERTITE, penitent
747 'SCAPES, misdeeds
755 IN, into
774 PROPORTION'D, regular
781 PRICK, hour-mark on dial
791 PALMERS, pilgrims
811 CIPHER, decipher
812 COTE, discern

line

820 SENSELESS, insensible
828 CREST-WOUNDING, blotting the scutcheon
830 MOT, motto
859 BARNS, *verb*
892 SMOOTHING, flattering
899 SORT, choose
920 SHIFT, evasion, trick
925 COPESMATE, accomplice
926 POST, messenger
936 FINE, end
985 ORTS, scraps
1013 SIGHTLESS, in which one does not see
1026 CONFIRM'D DESPITE, established disgrace
1046 FALCHION, sword
1050 TYPE, title
1062 GRAFF, graft
1070 DISPENSE WITH, pardon
1084 CLOUDY, sad
1094 FOND, foolish
1133 BURDEN, bass-undersong
1139 WINK, close
1140 FRETS, cross-bars on which string of a lute were stopped
1143 SHAMING, being ashamed
1167 PILL'D, stripped
1198 ABRIDGEMENT, abstract
1205 OVERSEE, be executor of
1206 OVERSEEN, deceived
1221 SORTS, suits
1222 FOR WHY, because
1257 HILD, held
1298 CONCEIT, meditation

The Phœnix and Turtle

Contents

VENUS & ADONIS

Vilia miretur vulgus; mihi flavus Apollo
Pocula Castalia plena ministret aqua.

To the

RIGHT HONORABLE HENRIE WRIOTHESLEY,

Earle of Southampton, and Baron of Titchfield.

RIGHT HONOURABLE,

I KNOW *not how I shall offend in dedicating my vnpolisht lines to your Lordship, nor how the worlde will censure me for choosing so strong a proppe to support so weake a burthen, onely if your Honour seeme but pleased, I account my selfe highly praised, and vowe to take aduantage of all idle houres, till I haue honoured you with some grauer labour. But if the first heire of my inuention proue deformed, I shall be sorie it had so noble a godfather : and neuer after eare so barren a land, for fear it yeeld me still so bad a haruest, I leaue it to your Honourable suruey, and your Honor to your hearts content, which I wish may alwaies answere your owne wish, and the worlds hopefull expectation.*

Your Honors in all dutie, William Shakespeare.

VENUS & ADONIS

Even as the sun with purple-colour'd face
Had ta'en his last leave of the weeping morn,
Rose-cheek'd Adonis hied him to the chase ;
Hunting he lov'd, but love he laugh'd to scorn :
 Sick-thoughted Venus makes amain unto him,
 And like a bold-fac'd suitor 'gins to woo him.

' Thrice fairer than myself,' (thus she began)
' The field's chief flower, sweet above compare,
Stain to all nymphs, more lovely than a man,
More white and red than doves or roses are ;   10
 Nature that made thee with herself at strife
 Saith that the world hath ending with thy life.

'Vouchsafe, thou wonder, to alight thy steed,
And rein his proud head to the saddle-bow;
If thou wilt deign this favour, for thy meed
A thousand honey secrets shalt thou know:
    Here come and sit, where never serpent hisses,
    And being set, I'll smother thee with kisses.

'And yet not cloy thy lips with loath'd satiety,
But rather famish them amid their plenty,   20
Making them red, and pale, with fresh variety;
Ten kisses short as one, one long as twenty:
    A summer's day will seem an hour but short,
    Being wasted in such time-beguiling sport.'

With this she seizeth on his sweating palm,
The precedent of pith and livelihood,
And, trembling in her passion, calls it balm,
Earth's sovereign salve, to do a goddess good:
    Being so enrag'd, desire doth lend her force
    Courageously to pluck him from his horse.   30

Over one arm the lusty courser's rein,
Under her other was the tender boy,
Who blush'd, and pouted in a dull disdain,
With leaden appetite, unapt to toy ;
  She red and hot as coals of glowing fire,
  He red for shame, but frosty in desire.

The studded bridle on a ragged bough
Nimbly she fastens—O, how quick is love !—
The steed is stalled up, and even now
To tie the rider she begins to prove :   40
  Backward she push'd him, as she would be thrust,
  And govern'd him in strength, though not in lust.

So soon was she along, as he was down,
Each leaning on their elbows and their hips :
Now doth she stroke his cheek, now doth he frown,
And 'gins to chide, but soon she stops his lips ;
  And kissing speaks, with lustful language broken,
  ' If thou wilt chide, thy lips shall never open.'

He burns with bashful shame, she with her tears
Doth quench the maiden burning of his cheeks,　　　　50
Then with her windy sighs, and golden hairs,
To fan and blow them dry again she seeks :
　　　He saith she is immodest, blames her miss ;
　　　What follows more she murders with a kiss.

Even as an empty eagle, sharp by fast,
Tires with her beak on feathers, flesh, and bone,
Shaking her wings, devouring all in haste,
Till either gorge be stuff'd, or prey be gone ;
　　　Even so she kiss'd his brow, his cheek, his chin,
　　　And where she ends, she doth anew begin.　　　60

Forc'd to content, but never to obey,
Panting he lies, and breatheth in her face ;
She feedeth on the steam, as on a prey,
And calls it heavenly moisture, air of grace ;
　　　Wishing her cheeks were gardens full of flowers,
　　　So they were dew'd with such distilling showers.

Look how a bird lies tangled in a net,
So fasten'd in her arms Adonis lies;
Pure shame and aw'd resistance made him fret,
Which bred more beauty in his angry eyes: 70
    Rain added to a river that is rank
    Perforce will force it overflow the bank.

Still she entreats, and prettily entreats,
For to a pretty ear she tunes her tale;
Still is he sullen, still he lours and frets,
'Twixt crimson shame, and anger ashy-pale;
    Being red, she loves him best, and being white,
    Her best is better'd with a more delight.

Look how he can, she cannot choose but love,
And by her fair immortal hand she swears,   80
From his soft bosom never to remove,
Till he take truce with her contending tears,
    Which long have rain'd, making her cheeks all wet;
    And one sweet kiss shall pay his countless debt.

Upon this promise did he raise his chin,
Like a dive-dapper peering through a wave,
Who, being look'd on, ducks as quickly in ;
So offers he to give what she did crave,
    But when her lips were ready for his pay,
    He winks, and turns his lips another way.   90

Never did passenger in summer's heat
More thirst for drink than she for this good turn ;
Her help she sees, but help she cannot get,
She bathes in water, yet her fire must burn :
    ' O, pity,' 'gan she cry, ' flint-hearted boy !
    'Tis but a kiss I beg, why art thou coy ?

' I have been woo'd, as I entreat thee now,
Even by the stern and direful god of war,
Whose sinewy neck in battle ne'er did bow,
Who conquers where he comes in every jar ;   100
    Yet hath he been my captive, and my slave,
    And begg'd for that which thou unask'd shalt have.

' Over my altars hath he hung his lance,
His batter'd shield, his uncontrolled crest,
And for my sake hath learn'd to sport, and dance,
To toy, to wanton, dally, smile, and jest,
  Scorning his churlish drum, and ensign red,
  Making my arms his field, his tent my bed.

' Thus he that overrul'd I oversway'd,
Leading him prisoner in a red rose chain ;   110
Strong-temper'd steel his stronger strength obeyed,
Yet was he servile to my coy disdain ;
  O, be not proud, nor brag not of thy might,
  For mastering her that foil'd the god of fight !

' Touch but my lips with those fair lips of thine—
Though mine be not so fair, yet are they red—
The kiss shall be thine own as well as mine :
What see'st thou in the ground ? hold up thy head,
  Look in mine eyeballs, there thy beauty lies,
  Then why not lips on lips, since eyes in eyes ?   120

7

' Is thine own heart to thine own face affected ?
Can thy right hand seize love upon thy left ?   †
Then woo thyself, be of thyself rejected,
Steal thine own freedom, and complain on theft.   160
    Narcissus so himself himself forsook,
    And died to kiss his shadow in the brook.

' Torches are made to light, jewels to wear,
Dainties to taste, fresh beauty for the use,
Herbs for their smell, and sappy plants to bear ;
Things growing to themselves are growth's abuse :
    Seeds spring from seeds, and beauty breedeth beauty ;
    Thou wast begot ; to get it is thy duty.

' Upon the earth's increase why shouldst thou feed,
Unless the earth with thy increase be fed ?   170
By law of nature thou art bound to breed,
That thine may live, when thou thyself art dead ;
    And so, in spite of death, thou dost survive,
    In that thy likeness still is left alive.'

By this, the love-sick queen began to sweat,
For, where they lay, the shadow had forsook them,
And Titan, tired in the mid-day heat,
With burning eye did hotly overlook them,
　　Wishing Adonis had his team to guide,
　　So he were like him, and by Venus' side.　　180

And now Adonis, with a lazy spright,
And with a heavy, dark, disliking eye,
His louring brows o'erwhelming his fair sight,
Like misty vapours when they blot the sky,
　　Souring his cheeks, cries, ' Fie, no more of love !
　　The sun doth burn my face, I must remove.'

' Ay me,' quoth Venus, ' young, and so unkind,
What bare excuses mak'st thou to be gone !
I 'll sigh celestial breath, whose gentle wind
Shall cool the heat of this descending sun :　　190
　　I 'll make a shadow for thee of my hairs,
　　If they burn too, I 'll quench them with my tears.

' The sun that shines from heaven shines but warm,
And, lo, I lie between that sun and thee :
The heat I have from thence doth little harm,
Thine eye darts forth the fire that burneth me ;
    And were I not immortal, life were done
    Between this heavenly and earthly sun.

' Art thou obdurate, flinty, hard as steel ?
Nay, more than flint, for stone at rain relenteth :   200
Art thou a woman's son, and canst not feel
What 'tis to love ? how want of love tormenteth ?
    O, had thy mother borne so hard a mind,
    She had not brought forth thee, but died unkind.

' What am I, that thou shouldst contemn me this ?
Or what great danger dwells upon my suit ?
What were thy lips the worse for one poor kiss ?
Speak, fair, but speak fair words, or else be mute :
    Give me one kiss, I 'll give it thee again,
    And one for interest, if thou wilt have twain.   210

' Fie, lifeless picture, cold and senseless stone.
Well painted idol, image dull, and dead,
Statue contenting but the eye alone,
Thing like a man, but of no woman bred !
    Thou art no man, though of a man's complexion,
    For men will kiss even by their own direction.'

This said, impatience chokes her pleading tongue,
And swelling passion doth provoke a pause ;
Red cheeks and fiery eyes blaze forth her wrong ;
Being judge in love, she cannot right her cause :   220
    And now she weeps, and now she fain would speak,
    And now her sobs do her intendments break.

Sometime she shakes her head, and then his hand,
Now gazeth she on him, now on the ground ;
Sometime her arms infold him like a band :
She would, he will not in her arms be bound ;
    And when from thence he struggles to be gone,
    She locks her lily fingers one in one.

'Fondling,' she saith, 'since I have hemm'd thee here
Within the circuit of this ivory pale,   230
I'll be a park, and thou shalt be my dear;
Feed where thou wilt, on mountain, or in dale:
    Graze on my lips, and if those hills be dry,
    Stray lower, where the pleasant fountains lie.

'Within this limit is relief enough,
Sweet bottom-grass and high delightful plain,
Round rising hillocks, brakes obscure and rough,
To shelter thee from tempest and from rain:
    Then be my dear, since I am such a park,
    No dog shall rouse thee, though a thousand bark.'   240

At this Adonis smiles as in disdain,
That in each cheek appears a pretty dimple:
Love made those hollows, if himself were slain,
He might be buried in a tomb so simple;
    Foreknowing well, if there he came to lie,
    Why, there Love liv'd, and there he could not die.

These lovely caves, these round enchanting pits,
Open'd their mouths to swallow Venus' liking.
Being mad before, how doth she now for wits?
Struck dead at first, what needs a second striking?   250
    Poor queen of love, in thine own law forlorn,
    To love a cheek that smiles at thee in scorn!

Now which way shall she turn? what shall she say?
Her words are done, her woes the more increasing,
The time is spent, her object will away,
And from her twining arms doth urge releasing.
    'Pity,' she cries, 'some favour, some remorse!'
    Away he springs, and hasteth to his horse.

But, lo, from forth a copse that neighbours by,
A breeding jennet, lusty, young, and proud,   260
Adonis' trampling courser doth espy;
And forth she rushes, snorts and neighs aloud:
    The strong-neck'd steed, being tied unto a tree,
    Breaketh his rein, and to her straight goes he.

Imperiously he leaps, he neighs, he bounds,
And now his woven girths he breaks asunder ;
The bearing earth with his hard hoof he wounds,
Whose hollow womb resounds like heaven's thunder ;
    The iron bit he crusheth 'tween his teeth,
    Controlling what he was controlled with.   270

His ears up-prick'd, his braided hanging mane
Upon his compass'd crest now stand on end,
His nostrils drink the air, and forth again,
As from a furnace, vapours doth he send :
    His eye, which scornfully glisters like fire,
    Shows his hot courage, and his high desire.

Sometime he trots, as if he told the steps,
With gentle majesty, and modest pride ;
Anon he rears upright, curvets, and leaps,
As who should say ' Lo, thus my strength is tried ;   280
    And this I do to captivate the eye
    Of the fair breeder that is standing by.'

What recketh he his rider's angry stir,
His flattering ' Holla ' or his ' Stand, I say ' ?
What cares he now for curb, or pricking spur,
For rich caparisons, or trappings gay ?
    He sees his love, and nothing else he sees,
    For nothing else with his proud sight agrees.

Look, when a painter would surpass the life,
In limning out a well proportion'd steed,   290
His art with nature's workmanship at strife,
As if the dead the living should exceed ;
    So did this horse excel a common one
    In shape, in courage, colour, pace and bone.

Round-hoof'd, short-jointed, fetlocks shag and long.
Broad breast, full eye, small head, and nostril wide,
High crest, short ears, straight legs, and passing strong,
Thin mane, thick tail, broad buttock, tender hide :
    Look what a horse should have, he did not lack,
    Save a proud rider on so proud a back.   300

Sometime he scuds far off, and there he stares ;
Anon he starts at stirring of a feather ;
To bid the wind a base he now prepares,
And whe'er he run, or fly, they know not whether ;
    For through his mane and tail the high wind sings,
    Fanning the hairs, who wave like feather'd wings.

He looks upon his love, and neighs unto her,
She answers him, as if she knew his mind,
Being proud, as females are, to see him woo her,
She puts on outward strangeness, seems unkind,   310
    Spurns at his love, and scorns the heat he feels,
    Beating his kind embracements with her heels.

Then, like a melancholy malcontent,
He vails his tail, that, like a falling plume,
Cool shadow to his melting buttock lent ;
He stamps, and bites the poor flies in his fume.
    His love, perceiving how he was enrag'd,
    Grew kinder, and his fury was assuag'd.

His testy master goeth about to take him,
When, lo, the unback'd breeder, full of fear,   320
Jealous of catching, swiftly doth forsake him,
With her the horse, and left Adonis there :
    As they were mad, unto the wood they hie them,
    Out-stripping crows that strive to over-fly them.

All swoln with chafing, down Adonis sits,
Banning his boisterous and unruly beast ;
And now the happy season once more fits,
That love-sick Love by pleading may be blest ;
    For lovers say, the heart hath treble wrong
    When it is barr'd the aidance of the tongue.   330

An oven that is stopp'd, or river stay'd,
Burneth more hotly, swelleth with more rage :
So of concealed sorrow may be said ;
Free vent of words love's fire doth assuage ;
    But when the heart's attorney once is mute,
    The client breaks, as desperate in his suit.

He sees her coming, and begins to glow,
Even as a dying coal revives with wind,
And with his bonnet hides his angry brow,
Looks on the dull earth with disturbed mind,   340
    Taking no notice that she is so nigh,
    For all askance he holds her in his eye.

O, what a sight it was wistly to view
How she came stealing to the wayward boy,
To note the fighting conflict of her hue,
How white and red each other did destroy !
    But now her cheek was pale, and by and by
    It flash'd forth fire, as lightning from the sky.

Now was she just before him as he sat,
And like a lowly lover down she kneels ;   350
With one fair hand she heaveth up his hat,
Her other tender hand his fair cheek feels :
    His tenderer cheek receives her soft hand's print,
    As apt as new-fall'n snow takes any dint.

O, what a war of looks was then between them !
Her eyes petitioners to his eyes suing,
His eyes saw her eyes as they had not seen them,
Her eyes woo'd still, his eyes disdain'd the wooing :
    And all this dumb play had his acts made plain
    With tears, which chorus-like her eyes did rain.   360

Full gently now she takes him by the hand,
A lily prison'd in a gaol of snow,
Or ivory in an alabaster band,
So white a friend engirts so white a foe :
    This beauteous combat, wilful and unwilling,
    Show'd like two silver doves that sit a-billing.

Once more the engine of her thoughts began :
' O fairest mover on this mortal round,
Would thou wert as I am, and I a man,
My heart all whole as thine, thy heart my wound,   370
    For one sweet look thy help I would assure thee,
    Though nothing but my body's bane would cure thee.'

'Give me my hand,' saith he ; ' why dost thou feel it ? '
'Give me my heart,' saith she, ' and thou shalt have it ;
O, give it me, lest thy hard heart do steel it,
And being steel'd, soft sighs can never grave it :
    Then love's deep groans I never shall regard,
    Because Adonis' heart hath made mine hard.'

'For shame,' he cries, ' let go, and let me go,
My day's delight is past, my horse is gone,   380
And 'tis your fault I am bereft him so ;
I pray you hence, and leave me here alone,
    For all my mind, my thought, my busy care,
    Is how to get my palfrey from the mare.'

Thus she replies : ' Thy palfrey, as he should,
Welcomes the warm approach of sweet desire :
Affection is a coal that must be cool'd,
Else, suffer'd, it will set the heart on fire :
    The sea hath bounds, but deep desire hath none ;
    Therefore no marvel though thy horse be gone.   390

' How like a jade he stood tied to the tree,
Servilely master'd with a leathern rein !
But when he saw his love, his youth's fair fee,
He held such petty bondage in disdain ;
    Throwing the base thong from his bending crest,
    Enfranchising his mouth, his back, his breast.

' Who sees his true-love in her naked bed,
Teaching the sheets a whiter hue than white,
But, when his glutton eye so full hath fed,
His other agents aim at like delight ?   400
    Who is so faint, that dares not be so bold
    To touch the fire, the weather being cold ?

' Let me excuse thy courser, gentle boy ;
And learn of him, I heartily beseech thee,
To take advantage on presented joy ;
Though I were dumb, yet his proceedings teach thee :
    O, learn to love, the lesson is but plain,
    And once made perfect, never lost again.'

' I know not love,' quoth he, ' nor will not know it,
Unless it be a boar, and then I chase it ;   410
'Tis much to borrow, and I will not owe it ;
My love to love is love but to disgrace it ;
    For I have heard it is a life in death,
      That laughs, and weeps, and all but with a breath.

' Who wears a garment shapeless and unfinish'd ?
Who plucks the bud before one leaf put forth ?
If springing things be any jot diminish'd,
They wither in their prime, prove nothing worth :
    The colt that 's back'd and burthen'd being young
      Loseth his pride, and never waxeth strong.   420

' You hurt my hand with wringing ; let us part,
And leave this idle theme, this bootless chat,
Remove your siege from my unyielding heart,
To love's alarms it will not ope the gate ;
    Dismiss your vows, your feigned tears, your flattery ;
      For where a heart is hard they make no battery.'

' What ! canst thou talk ? ' quoth she, ' hast thou a tongue ?
O, would thou hadst not, or I had no hearing !
Thy mermaid's voice hath done me double wrong ;
I had my load before, now press'd with bearing :   430
    Melodious discord, heavenly tune harsh-sounding,
    Ear's deep sweet music, and heart's deep sore wounding.

' Had I no eyes but ears, my ears would love
That inward beauty and invisible,
Or were I deaf, thy outward parts would move
Each part in me that were but sensible :
    Though neither eyes nor ears, to hear nor see,
    Yet should I be in love by touching thee.

' Say, that the sense of feeling were bereft me,
And that I could not see, nor hear, nor touch,   440
And nothing but the very smell were left me,
Yet would my love to thee be still as much ;
    For from the stillitory of thy face excelling
    Comes breath perfumed, that breedeth love by smelling.

'But, O, what banquet were thou to the taste,
Being nurse and feeder of the other four!
Would they not wish the feast might ever last,
And bid suspicion double-lock the door,
    Lest jealousy, that sour unwelcome guest,
    Should by his stealing in disturb the feast?'   450

Once more the ruby-colour'd portal open'd,
Which to his speech did honey passage yield;
Like a red morn, that ever yet betoken'd
Wreck to the seaman, tempest to the field,
    Sorrow to shepherds, woe unto the birds,
    Gusts, and foul flaws, to herdmen and to herds.

This ill presage advisedly she marketh:
Even as the wind is hush'd before it raineth,
Or as the wolf doth grin before he barketh,
Or as the berry breaks before it staineth,   460
    Or like the deadly bullet of a gun,
    His meaning struck her ere his words begun.

And at his look she flatly falleth down,
For looks kill love, and love by looks reviveth :
A smile recures the wounding of a frown ;
But blessed bankrupt, that by love so thriveth !
    The silly boy, believing she is dead,
    Claps her pale cheek, till clapping makes it red ;

And all amaz'd brake off his late intent,
For sharply he did think to reprehend her,   470
Which cunning love did wittily prevent :
Fair fall the wit that can so well defend her !
    For on the grass she lies as she were slain,
    Till his breath breatheth life in her again.

He wrings her nose, he strikes her on the cheeks,
He bends her fingers, holds her pulses hard,
He chafes her lips, a thousand ways he seeks
To mend the hurt that his unkindness marr'd :
    He kisses her, and she, by her good will,
    Will never rise, so he will kiss her still.   480

The night of sorrow now is turn'd to day :
Her two blue windows faintly she up-heaveth,
Like the fair sun, when in his fresh array
He cheers the morn, and all the earth relieveth :
    And as the bright sun glorifies the sky,
    So is her face illumin'd with her eye ;

Whose beams upon his hairless face are fix'd,
As if from thence they borrow'd all their shine.
Were never four such lamps, together mix'd,
Had not his clouded with his brow's repine ;   490
    But hers, which through the crystal tears gave light,
    Shone like the moon in water seen by night.

' O, where am I ? ' quoth she ; ' in earth or heaven,
Or in the ocean drench'd, or in the fire ?
What hour is this ? or morn or weary even ?
Do I delight to die, or life desire ?
    But now I liv'd, and life was death's annoy ;
    But now I died, and death was lively joy.

' O, thou didst kill me, kill me once again ;
Thy eyes' shrewd tutor, that hard heart of thine,   500
Hath taught them scornful tricks, and such disdain,
That they have murder'd this poor heart of mine,
    And these mine eyes, true leaders to their queen,
    But for thy piteous lips no more had seen.

' Long may they kiss each other, for this cure !
O, never let their crimson liveries wear !
And as they last, their verdure still endure,
To drive infection from the dangerous year !
    That the star-gazers, having writ on death,
    May say, the plague is banish'd by thy breath.   510

' Pure lips, sweet seals in my soft lips imprinted,
What bargains may I make still to be sealing ?
To sell myself I can be well contented,
So thou wilt buy, and pay, and use good dealing ;
    Which purchase if thou make, for fear of slips   †
    Set thy seal-manual on my wax-red lips.

' A thousand kisses buys my heart from me,
And pay them at thy leisure, one by one ;
What is ten hundred touches unto thee ?
Are they not quickly told and quickly gone ?   520
    Say for non-payment that the debt should double,
    Is twenty hundred kisses such a trouble ? '

' Fair queen,' quoth he, ' if any love you owe me,
Measure my strangeness with my unripe years ;
Before I know myself, seek not to know me ;
No fisher but the ungrown fry forbears :
    The mellow plum doth fall, the green sticks fast,
    Or, being early pluck'd, is sour to taste.

' Look, the world's comforter, with weary gait,
His day's hot task hath ended in the west ;   530
The owl, night's herald, shrieks, 'tis very late ;
The sheep are gone to fold, birds to their nest ;
    And coal-black clouds that shadow heaven's light
    Do summon us to part, and bid good night.

' Now let me say " Good night," and so say you ;
If you will say so, you shall have a kiss.'
' Good night,' quoth she ; and, ere he says ' Adieu,'
The honey fee of parting tender'd is :
     Her arms do lend his neck a sweet embrace,
     Incorporate then they seem, face grows to face.   540

Till breathless he disjoin'd, and backward drew
The heavenly moisture, that sweet coral mouth,
Whose precious taste her thirsty lips well knew,
Whereon they surfeit, yet complain on drouth :
     He with her plenty press'd, she faint with dearth,
     Their lips together glued, fall to the earth.

Now quick desire hath caught the yielding prey,
And glutton-like she feeds, yet never filleth ;
Her lips are conquerors, his lips obey,
Paying what ransom the insulter willeth ;   550
     Whose vulture thought doth pitch the price so high,
     That she will draw his lips' rich treasure dry.

And having felt the sweetness of the spoil,
With blindfold fury she begins to forage ;
Her face doth reek and smoke, her blood doth boil,
And careless lust stirs up a desperate courage,
> Planting oblivion, beating reason back,
> Forgetting shame's pure blush, and honour's wrack.

Hot, faint and weary, with her hard embracing,
Like a wild bird being tam'd with too much handling, 560
Or as the fleet-foot roe that's tir'd with chasing,
Or like the froward infant still'd with dandling,
> He now obeys, and now no more resisteth,
> While she takes all she can, not all she listeth.

What wax so frozen but dissolves with tempering,
And yields at last to every light impression ?
Things out of hope are compass'd oft with venturing,
Chiefly in love, whose leave exceeds commission :
> Affection faints not like a pale-fac'd coward,
> But then woos best when most his choice is froward.

When he did frown, O, had she then gave over,   571
Such nectar from his lips she had not suck'd ;
Foul words and frowns must not repel a lover ;
What though the rose have prickles, yet 'tis pluck'd :
    Were beauty under twenty locks kept fast,
    Yet love breaks through, and picks them all at last.

For pity now she can no more detain him ;
The poor fool prays her that he may depart :
She is resolv'd no longer to restrain him ;
Bids him farewell, and look well to her heart,   580
    The which, by Cupid's bow she doth protest,
    He carries thence incaged in his breast.

'Sweet boy,' she says, 'this night I'll waste in sorrow,
For my sick heart commands mine eyes to watch ;
Tell me, love's master, shall we meet to-morrow ?
Say, shall we? shall we? wilt thou make the match?'
    He tells her, no ; to-morrow he intends
    To hunt the boar with certain of his friends.

'The boar!' quoth she: whereat a sudden pale,
Like lawn being spread upon the blushing rose,   590
Usurps her cheek; she trembles at his tale,
And on his neck her yoking arms she throws:
    She sinketh down, still hanging by his neck,
    He on her belly falls, she on her back.

Now is she in the very lists of love,
Her champion mounted for the hot encounter:
All is imaginary she doth prove,
He will not manage her, although he mount her;
    That worse than Tantalus' is her annoy,   †
    To clip Elysium, and to lack her joy.   600

Even so poor birds, deceiv'd with painted grapes,
Do surfeit by the eye and pine the maw;
Even so she languisheth in her mishaps,
As those poor birds that helpless berries saw;
    The warm effects which she in him finds missing
    She seeks to kindle with continual kissing.

But all in vain, good queen, it will not be ;
She hath assay'd as much as may be prov'd ;
Her pleading hath deserv'd a greater fee ;
She's Love, she loves, and yet she is not lov'd.   610
    ' Fie, fie,' he says, ' you crush me ; let me go ;
    You have no reason to withhold me so.'

' Thou hadst been gone,' quoth she, ' sweet boy, ere this,
But that thou told'st me thou wouldst hunt the boar ;
O, be advis'd : thou know'st not what it is
With javelin's point a churlish swine to gore,
    Whose tushes never sheath'd he whetteth still,
    Like to a mortal butcher bent to kill.

' On his bow-back he hath a battle set
Of bristly pikes that ever threat his foes ;   620
His eyes like glow-worms shine when he doth fret,
His snout digs sepulchres where'er he goes ;
    Being mov'd, he strikes whate'er is in his way,
    And whom he strikes his crooked tushes slay.

' His brawny sides, with hairy bristles armed,
Are better proof than thy spear's point can enter;
His short thick neck cannot be easily harmed;
Being ireful, on the lion he will venture:
>> The thorny brambles, and embracing bushes,
>> As fearful of him, part, through whom he rushes.   630

' Alas, he nought esteems that face of thine,
To which Love's eyes pay tributary gazes;
Nor thy soft hands, sweet lips and crystal eyne,
Whose full perfection all the world amazes;
>> But having thee at vantage—wondrous dread!—
>> Would root these beauties as he roots the mead.

' O, let him keep his loathsome cabin still;
Beauty hath nought to do with such foul fiends:
Come not within his danger by thy will;
They that thrive well take counsel of their friends.   640
>> When thou didst name the boar, not to dissemble,
>> I fear'd thy fortune, and my joints did tremble.

' Didst thou not mark my face ? was it not white ?
Saw'st thou not signs of fear lurk in mine eye ?
Grew I not faint ? and fell I not downright ?
Within my bosom, whereon thou dost lie,
> My boding heart pants, beats, and takes no rest,
> But, like an earthquake, shakes thee on my breast.

' For where Love reigns, disturbing Jealousy
Doth call himself Affection's sentinel ;   650
Gives false alarms, suggested mutiny,
And in a peaceful hour doth cry " Kill, kill ! "
> Distempering gentle love in his desire,
> As air and water do abate the fire.

' This sour informer, this bate-breeding spy,
This canker that eats up love's tender spring,
This carry-tale, dissentious jealousy,
That sometime true news, sometime false doth bring,
> Knocks at my heart, and whispers in mine ear,
> That if I love thee, I thy death should fear :   660

' And more than so, presenteth to mine eye
The picture of an angry chafing boar,
Under whose sharp fangs on his back doth lie
An image like thyself, all stain'd with gore,
    Whose blood upon the fresh flowers being shed
    Doth make them droop with grief, and hang the head.

' What should I do, seeing thee so indeed,
That tremble at the imagination ?
The thought of it doth make my faint heart bleed,
And fear doth teach it divination :   670
    I prophesy thy death, my living sorrow,
    If thou encounter with the boar to-morrow.

' But if thou needs wilt hunt, be rul'd by me ;
Uncouple at the timorous flying hare,
Or at the fox which lives by subtlety,
Or at the roe which no encounter dare :
    Pursue these fearful creatures o'er the downs,
    And on thy well-breath'd horse keep with thy hounds.

' And when thou hast on foot the purblind hare,
Mark the poor wretch, to overshoot his troubles,   680
How he outruns the wind, and with what care
He cranks and crosses with a thousand doubles :
    The many musits through the which he goes
    Are like a labyrinth to amaze his foes.

' Sometime he runs among a flock of sheep,
To make the cunning hounds mistake their smell,
And sometime where earth-delving conies keep,
To stop the loud pursuers in their yell ;
    And sometime sorteth with a herd of deer ;
    Danger deviseth shifts, wit waits on fear :   690

' For there his smell with others being mingled,
The hot scent-snuffing hounds are driven to doubt,
Ceasing their clamorous cry, till they have singled
With much ado the cold fault cleanly out ;
    Then do they spend their mouths, Echo replies,
    As if another chase were in the skies.

' By this, poor Wat, far off upon a hill,
Stands on his hinder legs with listening ear,
To hearken if his foes pursue him still ;
Anon their loud alarums he doth hear,   700
     And now his grief may be compared well
     To one sore sick that hears the passing-bell.

' Then shalt thou see the dew-bedabbled wretch
Turn, and return, indenting with the way ;   †
Each envious brier his weary legs doth scratch,
Each shadow makes him stop, each murmur stay,
     For misery is trodden on by many,
     And, being low, never reliev'd by any.

' Lie quietly, and hear a little more ;
Nay, do not struggle, for thou shalt not rise :   710
To make thee hate the hunting of the boar,
Unlike myself thou hear'st me moralize,
     Applying this to that, and so to so ;
     For love can comment upon every woe.

' Where did I leave ? ' ' No matter where,' quoth he ;
' Leave me, and then the story aptly ends :
The night is spent.' ' Why, what of that ? ' quoth she.
' I am,' quoth he, ' expected of my friends,
 And now 'tis dark, and going I shall fall.'
  ' In night,' quoth she, ' desire sees best of all. 720

' But if thou fall, O, then imagine this,
The earth, in love with thee, thy footing trips,
And all is but to rob thee of a kiss.
Rich preys make true men thieves ; so do thy lips
 Make modest Dian cloudy and forlorn,
  Lest she should steal a kiss, and die forsworn.

' Now of this dark night I perceive the reason :
Cynthia for shame obscures her silver shine,
Till forging Nature be condemn'd of treason,
For stealing moulds from heaven that were divine ; 730
 Wherein she fram'd thee, in high heaven's despite,
  To shame the sun by day, and her by night.

'And therefore hath she brib'd the Destinies
To cross the curious workmanship of nature,
To mingle beauty with infirmities
And pure perfection with impure defeature,
 Making it subject to the tyranny
  Of mad mischances and much misery;

'As burning fevers, agues pale and faint,
Life-poisoning pestilence, and frenzies wood,   740
The marrow-eating sickness, whose attaint
Disorder breeds by heating of the blood:
 Surfeits, imposthumes, grief, and damn'd despair,
  Swear Nature's death for framing thee so fair.

'And not the least of all these maladies
But in one minute's fight brings beauty under:
Both favour, savour, hue, and qualities,
Whereat the impartial gazer late did wonder,
 Are on the sudden wasted, thaw'd, and done,
  As mountain snow melts with the midday sun. 750

' Therefore, despite of fruitless chastity,
Love-lacking vestals and self-loving nuns,
That on the earth would breed a scarcity
And barren dearth of daughters and of sons,
  Be prodigal ; the lamp that burns by night
  Dries up his oil to lend the world his light.

' What is thy body but a swallowing grave,
Seeming to bury that posterity
Which by the rights of time thou needs must have,
If thou destroy them not in dark obscurity ? 760
  If so, the world will hold thee in disdain,
  Sith in thy pride so fair a hope is slain.

' So in thyself thyself art made away,
A mischief worse than civil home-bred strife,
Or theirs whose desperate hands themselves do slay,
Or butcher-sire that reaves his son of life.
  Foul cankering rust the hidden treasure frets,
  But gold that's put to use more gold begets.'

' Nay, then,' quoth Adon, ' you will fall again
Into your idle over-handled theme ; 770
The kiss I gave you is bestow'd in vain,
And all in vain you strive against the stream ;
 For, by this black-fac'd night, desire's foul nurse,
 Your treatise makes me like you worse and worse.

' If love have lent you twenty thousand tongues,
And every tongue more moving than your own,
Bewitching like the wanton mermaid's songs,
Yet from mine ear the tempting tune is blown ;
 For know, my heart stands armed in mine ear,
 And will not let a false sound enter there ; 780

' Lest the deceiving harmony should run
Into the quiet closure of my breast,
And then my little heart were quite undone,
In his bedchamber to be barr'd of rest ;
 No, lady, no ; my heart longs not to groan,
 But soundly sleeps, while now it sleeps alone.

44

' What have you urg'd that I cannot reprove ?
The path is smooth that leadeth on to danger ;
I hate not love, but your device in love
That lends embracements unto every stranger.   790
    You do it for increase : O strange excuse,
    When reason is the bawd to lust's abuse !

' Call it not love, for Love to heaven is fled
Since sweating Lust on earth usurp'd his name ;
Under whose simple semblance he hath fed
Upon fresh beauty, blotting it with blame ;
    Which the hot tyrant stains, and soon bereaves,
    As caterpillars do the tender leaves.

' Love comforteth like sunshine after rain,
But Lust's effect is tempest after sun ;   800
Love's gentle spring doth always fresh remain,
Lust's winter comes ere summer half be done ;
    Love surfeits not, Lust like a glutton dies ;
    Love is all truth, Lust full of forged lies.

' More I could tell, but more I dare not say,
The text is old, the orator too green,
Therefore in sadness now I will away,
My face is full of shame, my heart of teen,
 Mine ears, that to your wanton talk attended,
 Do burn themselves for having so offended.' 810

With this, he breaketh from the sweet embrace
Of those fair arms which bound him to her breast,
And homeward through the dark lawnd runs apace,
Leaves Love upon her back, deeply distress'd ;
 Look, how a bright star shooteth from the sky,
 So glides he in the night from Venus' eye :

Which after him she darts, as one on shore
Gazing upon a late-embarked friend,
Till the wild waves will have him seen no more,
Whose ridges with the meeting clouds contend : 820
 So did the merciless and pitchy night
 Fold in the object that did feed her sight.

Whereat amaz'd, as one that unaware
Hath dropp'd a precious jewel in the flood,
Or 'stonish'd, as night-wanderers often are,
Their light blown out in some mistrustful wood ;
    Even so confounded in the dark she lay,
    Having lost the fair discovery of her way.

And now she beats her heart, whereat it groans,
That all the neighbour caves, as seeming troubled,   830
Make verbal repetition of her moans ;
Passion on passion deeply is redoubled :
    ' Ay me ! ' she cries, and twenty times, ' Woe, woe ! '
    And twenty echoes twenty times cry so.

She, marking them, begins a wailing note,
And sings extemporally a woeful ditty ;
How love makes young men thrall, and old men dote,
How love is wise in folly, foolish-witty :
    Her heavy anthem still concludes in woe,
    And still the choir of echoes answer so.   840

Her song was tedious, and outwore the night,
For lover's hours are long, though seeming short;
If pleas'd themselves, others, they think, delight
In such-like circumstance, with such-like sport:
  Their copious stories, oftentimes begun,
  End without audience, and are never done.

For who hath she to spend the night withal,
But idle sounds resembling parasites;
Like shrill-tongued tapsters answering every call,
Soothing the humour of fantastic wits?   850
  She says ''Tis so': they answer all ''Tis so';
  And would say after her, if she said 'No.'

Lo, here the gentle lark, weary of rest,
From his moist cabinet mounts up on high,
And wakes the morning, from whose silver breast
The sun ariseth in his majesty;
  Who doth the world so gloriously behold,
  That cedar-tops and hills seem burnish'd gold.

Venus salutes him with this fair good-morrow:
' O thou clear god, and patron of all light,   860
From whom each lamp and shining star doth borrow
The beauteous influence that makes him bright,
 There lives a son that suck'd an earthly mother
 May lend thee light, as thou dost lend to other.'

This said, she hasteth to a myrtle grove,
Musing the morning is so much o'erworn,
And yet she hears no tidings of her love;
She hearkens for his hounds and for his horn,
 Anon she hears them chant it lustily,
 And all in haste she coasteth to the cry.   870

And as she runs, the bushes in the way
Some catch her by the neck, some kiss her face,
Some twine about her thigh to make her stay,
She wildly breaketh from their strict embrace,
 Like a milch doe, whose swelling dugs do ache
 Hasting to feed her fawn hid in some brake.

By this she hears the hounds are at a bay,
Whereat she starts, like one that spies an adder
Wreath'd up in fatal folds just in his way,
The fear whereof doth make him shake and shudder;   880
    Even so the timorous yelping of the hounds
    Appals her senses and her spirit confounds.

For now she knows it is no gentle chase,
But the blunt boar, rough bear, or lion proud,
Because the cry remaineth in one place,
Where fearfully the dogs exclaim aloud,
    Finding their enemy to be so curst,
    They all strain courtesy who shall cope him first.

This dismal cry rings sadly in her ear,
Through which it enters to surprise her heart,   890
Who, overcome by doubt and bloodless fear,
With cold-pale weakness numbs each feeling part,
    Like soldiers, when their captain once doth yield,
    They basely fly, and dare not stay the field.

Thus stands she in a trembling ecstasy ;
Till, cheering up her senses all dismay'd,
She tells them 'tis a causeless fantasy,
And childish error, that they are afraid,
    Bids them leave quaking, bids them fear no more :
    And with that word she spied the hunted boar ;   900

Whose frothy mouth, bepainted all with red,
Like milk and blood being mingled both together,
A second fear through all her sinews spread,
Which madly hurries her she knows not whither :
    This way she runs, and now she will no further,
    But back retires, to rate the boar for murther.

A thousand spleens bear her a thousand ways ;
She treads the path that she untreads again ;
Her more than haste is mated with delays,
Like the proceedings of a drunken brain,   910
    Full of respects, yet not at all respecting,
    In hand with all things, nought at all effecting.

Here kennell'd in a brake she finds a hound,
And asks the weary caitiff for his master,
And there another licking of his wound,
'Gainst venom'd sores the only sovereign plaster;
    And here she meets another, sadly scowling,
     To whom she speaks, and he replies with howling.

When he hath ceas'd his ill-resounding noise,
Another flap-mouth'd mourner, black, and grim,   920
Against the welkin volleys out his voice,
Another, and another, answer him,
    Clapping their proud tails to the ground below,
     Shaking their scratch'd ears, bleeding as they go.

Look, how the world's poor people are amazed
At apparitions, signs, and prodigies,
Whereon with fearful eyes they long have gazed,
Infusing them with dreadful prophecies;
    So she at these sad signs draws up her breath,
     And, sighing it again, exclaims on death.   930

'Hard-favour'd tyrant, ugly, meagre, lean,
Hateful divorce of love,'—thus chides she death,—
'Grim-grinning ghost, earth's worm, what dost thou mean
To stifle beauty, and to steal his breath,
    Who when he liv'd, his breath and beauty set
    Gloss on the rose, smell to the violet?

'If he be dead,—O no, it cannot be,
Seeing his beauty, thou shouldst strike at it ;—
O yes, it may, thou hast no eyes to see,
But hatefully at random dost thou hit ;   940
    Thy mark is feeble age, but thy false dart
    Mistakes that aim, and cleaves an infant's heart.

'Hadst thou but bid beware, then he had spoke,
And, hearing him, thy power had lost his power ;
The Destinies will curse thee for this stroke ;
They bid thee crop a weed, thou pluck'st a flower ;
    Love's golden arrow at him should have fled,
    And not Death's ebon dart to strike him dead.

'Dost thou drink tears, that thou provok'st such weeping?
What may a heavy groan advantage thee? 950
Why hast thou cast into eternal sleeping
Those eyes that taught all other eyes to see?
  Now Nature cares not for thy mortal vigour,
  Since her best work is ruin'd with thy rigour.'

Here overcome, as one full of despair,
She vail'd her eyelids, who, like sluices, stopp'd
The crystal tide, that from her two cheeks fair
In the sweet channel of her bosom dropp'd;
  But through the flood-gates breaks the silver rain,
  And with his strong course opens them again. 960

O, how her eyes and tears did lend and borrow!
Her eye seen in the tears, tears in her eye,
Both crystals, where they view'd each other's sorrow;
Sorrow that friendly sighs sought still to dry,
  But like a stormy day, now wind, now rain,
  Sighs dry her cheeks, tears make them wet again.

Variable passions throng her constant woe,
As striving who should best become her grief;
All entertain'd, each passion labours so
That every present sorrow seemeth chief,   970
  But none is best: then join they all together,
  Like many clouds, consulting for foul weather.

By this, far off she hears some huntsman holloa;
A nurse's song ne'er pleased her babe so well:
The dire imagination she did follow
This sound of hope doth labour to expel;
  For now reviving joy bids her rejoice,
  And flatters her it is Adonis' voice.

Whereat her tears began to turn their tide,
Being prison'd in her eye like pearls in glass,   980
Yet sometimes falls an orient drop beside,
Which her cheek melts, as scorning it should pass
  To wash the foul face of the sluttish ground,
  Who is but drunken when she seemeth drown'd.

O hard-believing love, how strange it seems
Not to believe, and yet too credulous !
Thy weal and woe are both of them extremes,
Despair, and hope, makes thee ridiculous :
    The one doth flatter thee in thoughts unlikely,
    In likely thoughts the other kills thee quickly.   990

Now she unweaves the web that she hath wrought ;
Adonis lives, and Death is not to blame ;
It was not she that call'd him all to nought :
Now she adds honours to his hateful name ;
    She clepes him king of graves, and grave for kings,
    Imperious supreme of all mortal things.

' No, no,' quoth she, ' sweet Death, I did but jest,
Yet pardon me, I felt a kind of fear
Whenas I met the boar, that bloody beast,
Which knows no pity, but is still severe ;   1000
    Then, gentle shadow,—truth I must confess,—
    I rail'd on thee, fearing my love's decease.

' 'Tis not my fault, the boar provok'd my tongue,
Be wreak'd on him, invisible commander ;
'Tis he, foul creature, that hath done thee wrong,
I did but act, he 's author of thy slander :
    Grief hath two tongues, and never woman yet
    Could rule them both, without ten women's wit.'

Thus hoping that Adonis is alive,
Her rash suspect she doth extenuate,   1010
And that his beauty may the better thrive,
With Death she humbly doth insinuate ;
    Tells him of trophies, statues, tombs, and stories
    His victories, his triumphs, and his glories.

' O Jove,' quoth she, ' how much a fool was I
To be of such a weak and silly mind,
To wail his death who lives, and must not die,
Till mutual overthrow of mortal kind !
    For he being dead, with him is beauty slain,
    And, beauty dead, black Chaos comes again.   1020

' Fie, fie, fond love, thou art so full of fear
As one with treasure laden, hemm'd with thieves ;
Trifles unwitnessed with eye or ear
Thy coward heart with false bethinking grieves.'
    Even at this word she hears a merry horn,
    Whereat she leaps that was but late forlorn.

As falcons to the lure, away she flies ;
The grass stoops not, she treads on it so light,
And in her haste unfortunately spies
The foul boar's conquest on her fair delight ;   1030
    Which seen, her eyes, are murder'd with the view ;   †
    Like stars asham'd of day, themselves withdrew ;

Or, as the snail, whose tender horns being hit,
Shrinks backward in his shelly cave with pain,
And there all smother'd up in shade doth sit,
Long after fearing to creep forth again ;
    So, at his bloody view, her eyes are fled
    Into the deep-dark cabins of her head :

Where they resign their office and their light
To the disposing of her troubled brain,   1040
Who bids them still consort with ugly night,
And never wound the heart with looks again,
    Who, like a king perplexed in his throne,
    By their suggestion gives a deadly groan ;

Whereat each tributary subject quakes,
As when the wind, imprison'd in the ground,
Struggling for passage, earth's foundation shakes,
Which with cold terror doth men's minds confound.
    This mutiny each part doth so surprise,
    That from their dark beds once more leap her eyes ;

And being open'd threw unwilling light   1051
Upon the wide wound that the boar had trench'd
In his soft flank, whose wonted lily white
With purple tears, that his wound wept, was drench'd :
    No flower was nigh, no grass, herb, leaf or weed,
    But stole his blood, and seem'd with him to bleed.

This solemn sympathy poor Venus noteth ;
Over one shoulder doth she hang her head ;
Dumbly she passions, franticly she doteth ;
She thinks he could not die, he is not dead :   1060
    Her voice is stopp'd, her joints forget to bow,
    Her eyes are mad that they have wept till now.   †

Upon his hurt she looks so steadfastly
That her sight dazzling makes the wound seem three,   †
And then she reprehends her mangling eye,
That makes more gashes where no breach should be :
    His face seems twain, each several limb is doubled,
    For oft the eye mistakes, the brain being troubled.

' My tongue cannot express my grief for one,
And yet,' quoth she, ' behold two Adons dead !   1070
My sighs are blown away, my salt tears gone,
Mine eyes are turn'd to fire, my heart to lead ;
    Heavy heart's lead, melt at mine eyes' red fire !
    So shall I die by drops of hot desire.

' Alas, poor world, what treasure hast thou lost !
What face remains alive that's worth the viewing ?
Whose tongue is music now ? what canst thou boast
Of things long since, or any thing ensuing ?
    The flowers are sweet, their colours fresh and trim ;
    But true-sweet beauty liv'd and died with him.   1080

' Bonnet nor veil henceforth no creature wear !
Nor sun, nor wind, will ever strive to kiss you :
Having no fair to lose, you need not fear ;
The sun doth scorn you, and the wind doth hiss you :
    But when Adonis liv'd, sun and sharp air
    Lurk'd like two thieves, to rob him of his fair.

' And therefore would he put his bonnet on,
Under whose brim the gaudy sun would peep ;
The wind would blow it off, and, being gone,
Play with his locks ; then would Adonis weep ;   1090
    And straight, in pity of his tender years,
    They both would strive who first should dry his tears.

' To see his face the lion walk'd along
Behind some hedge, because he would not fear him ;
To recreate himself when he hath sung,
The tiger would be tame, and gently hear him ;
    If he had spoke, the wolf would leave his prey,
    And never fright the silly lamb that day.

' When he beheld his shadow in the brook,
The fishes spread on it their golden gills ;   1100
When he was by, the birds such pleasure took,
That some would sing, some other in their bills
    Would bring him mulberries and ripe-red cherries ;
    He fed them with his sight, they him with berries.

' But this foul, grim, and urchin-snouted boar,
Whose downward eye still looketh for a grave,
Ne'er saw the beauteous livery that he wore ;
Witness the entertainment that he gave :
    If he did see his face, why then I know
    He thought to kiss him, and hath kill'd him so.   1110

' 'Tis true, 'tis true, thus was Adonis slain ;
He ran upon the boar with his sharp spear,
Who did not whet his teeth at him again,
But by a kiss thought to persuade him there ;
 And nuzzling in his flank, the loving swine
 Sheath'd unaware the tusk in his soft groin.

' Had I been tooth'd like him, I must confess,
With kissing him I should have kill'd him first ;
But he is dead, and never did he bless
My youth with his, the more am I accurst.'   1120
 With this, she falleth in the place she stood,
 And stains her face with his congealed blood.

She looks upon his lips, and they are pale,
She takes him by the hand, and that is cold,
She whispers in his ears a heavy tale,
As if they heard the woeful words she told ;
 She lifts the coffer-lids that close his eyes,
 Where, lo, two lamps burnt out in darkness lies ;

Two glasses, where herself herself beheld
A thousand times, and now no more reflect; 1130
Their virtue lost, wherein they late excell'd,
And every beauty robb'd of his effect:
    ' Wonder of time,' quoth she, ' this is my spite,
      That, thou being dead, the day should yet be light.

' Since thou art dead, lo, here I prophesy,
Sorrow on love hereafter shall attend:
It shall be waited on with jealousy,
Find sweet beginning, but unsavoury end;
    Ne'er settled equally, but high or low,
      That all love's pleasure shall not match his woe. 1140

' It shall be fickle, false, and full of fraud,
Bud, and be blasted, in a breathing-while,
The bottom poison, and the top o'erstraw'd
With sweets that shall the truest sight beguile;
    The strongest body shall it make most weak,
      Strike the wise dumb, and teach the fool to speak.

' It shall be sparing, and too full of riot,
Teaching decrepit age to tread the measures,
The staring ruffian shall it keep in quiet,
Pluck down the rich, enrich the poor with treasures ;   1150
    It shall be raging-mad, and silly-mild,
    Make the young old, the old become a child.

' It shall suspect where is no cause of fear,
It shall not fear where it should most mistrust,
It shall be merciful, and too severe,
And most deceiving when it seems most just ;
    Perverse it shall be where it shows most toward,
    Put fear to valour, courage to the coward.

' It shall be cause of war, and dire events,
And set dissension 'twixt the son and sire,   1160
Subject and servile to all discontents,
As dry combustious matter is to fire ;
    Sith in his prime death doth my love destroy
    They that love best their loves shall not enjoy.'

VENUS AND ADONIS

By this the boy that by her side lay kill'd
Was melted like a vapour from her sight,
And in his blood, that on the ground lay spill'd,
A purple flower sprung up, chequer'd with white,
     Resembling well his pale cheeks, and the blood
      Which in round drops upon their whiteness stood.   1170

She bows her head, the new-sprung flower to smell,
Comparing it to her Adonis' breath,
And says, within her bosom it shall dwell,
Since he himself is reft from her by death :
     She crops the stalk, and in the breach appears
      Green-dropping sap, which she compares to tears.

'Poor flower,' quoth she, ' this way thy father's guise—
Sweet issue of a more sweet-smelling sire—
For every little grief to wet his eyes ;
To grow unto himself was his desire ;   1180
     And so 'tis thine, but know, it is as good
      To wither in my breast as in his blood.

' Here was thy father's bed, here in my breast,
Thou art the next of blood, and 'tis thy right :
Lo, in this hollow cradle take thy rest,
My throbbing heart shall rock thee day and night :
     There shall not be one minute in an hour
     Wherein I will not kiss my sweet love's flower.'

Thus weary of the world, away she hies,
And yokes her silver doves, by whose swift aid   1190
Their mistress mounted through the empty skies
In her light chariot quickly is convey'd ;
     Holding their course to Paphos, where their queen
     Means to immure herself, and not be seen.

LUCRECE

To the

RIGHT HONOURABLE, HENRY WRIOTHESLEY

Earle of Southhampton, and Baron of Titchfield.

*T*HE *loue I dedicate to your Lordship is without end :
whereof this Pamphlet without beginning is but a super-
fluous Moity. The warrant I haue of your Honourable disposition, not the worth of my vntutord Lines makes it assured of
acceptance. What I haue done is yours, what I haue to doe
is yours, being part in all I haue, deuoted yours. Were my
worth greater, my duety would shew greater, meane time, as
it is, it is bound to your Lordship ; To whom I wish long
life still lengthned with all happinesse.*

Your Lordships in all duety.

WILLIAM SHAKESPEARE.

THE ARGUMENT

LUCIUS TARQUINIUS, for his excessive pride surnamed Superbus, after he had caused his own father-in-law Servius Tullius to be cruelly murdered, and, contrary to the Roman laws and customs, not requiring or staying for the people's suffrages, had possessed himself of the kingdom, went, accompanied with his sons and other noblemen of Rome, to besiege Ardea, during which siege the principal men of the army meeting one evening at the tent of Sextus Tarquinius, the king's son, in their discourses after supper every one commended the virtues of his own wife; among whom Collatinus extolled the incomparable chastity of his wife Lucretia. In that pleasant humour they all posted to Rome, and intending by their secret and sudden arrival to make trial of that which every one had before avouched, only Collatinus finds his wife, though it were late in the night, spinning amongst her maids, the other ladies were all found dancing and revelling, or in several disports. Whereupon the noblemen yielded Collatinus the victory, and his wife the fame. At that time Sextus Tarquinius being inflamed with Lucrece' beauty, yet smothering his passions for the present, departed with the rest back to the camp; from whence he shortly after privily withdrew himself, and was, according to his estate, royally entertained and lodged by Lucrece at Collatium. The same night he treacherously stealeth into her chamber, violently ravished her, and early in the morning speedeth away. Lucrece, in this lamentable plight, hastily dispatcheth messengers, one to Rome for her father, another to the camp for Collatine. They came, the one accompanied with Junius Brutus, the other with Publius Valerius; and finding Lucrece attired in mourning habit, demanded the cause

71

of her sorrow. She, first taking an oath of them for her revenge, revealed the actor and whole manner of his dealing, and withal suddenly stabbed herself. Which done, with one consent they all vowed to root out the whole hated family of the Tarquins; and bearing the dead body to Rome, Brutus acquainted the people with the doer and manner of the vile deed, with a bitter invective against the tyranny of the king, wherewith the people were so moved, that with one consent and a general acclamation the Tarquins were all exiled, and the state government changed from kings to consuls.

THE RAPE OF LUCRECE

FROM the besieged Ardea all in post,
Borne by the trustless wings of false desire,
Lust-breathed Tarquin leaves the Roman host,
And to Collatium bears the lightless fire,
Which, in pale embers hid, lurks to aspire,
  And girdle with embracing flames the waist
  Of Collatine's fair love, Lucrece the chaste.

Hap'ly that name of 'chaste' unhapp'ly set   †
This bateless edge on his keen appetite ;
When Collatine unwisely did not let   10
To praise the clear unmatched red and white
Which triumph'd in that sky of his delight ;
  Where mortal stars, as bright as heaven's beauties,
  With pure aspects did him peculiar duties.

For he the night before, in Tarquin's tent,
Unlock'd the treasure of his happy state ;
What priceless wealth the heavens had him lent,
In the possession of his beauteous mate ;
Reckoning his fortune at such high-proud rate,   †
    That kings might be espoused to more fame,   20
    But king nor peer to such a peerless dame.

O happiness enjoy'd but of a few !
And, if possess'd, as soon decay'd and done
As is the morning silver melting dew   †
Against the golden splendour of the sun !
An expir'd date, cancell'd ere well begun :   †
    Honour and beauty, in the owner's arms,
    Are weakly fortress'd from a world of harms.

Beauty itself doth of itself persuade
The eyes of men without an orator ;   30
What needeth then apology be made,
To set forth that which is so singular ?
Or why is Collatine the publisher
    Of that rich jewel he should keep unknown
    From thievish ears, because it is his own ?

Perchance his boast of Lucrece' sovereignty
Suggested this proud issue of a king ;
For by our ears our hearts oft tainted be :
Perchance that envy of so rich a thing,
Braving compare, disdainfully did sting   · 40
    His high-pitch'd thoughts, that meaner men should
        vaunt
    That golden hap which their superiors want.

But some untimely thought did instigate
His all-too-timeless speed, if none of those :
His honour, his affairs, his friends, his state,
Neglected all, with swift intent he goes
To quench the coal which in his liver glows.
    O rash false heat, wrapp'd in repentant cold,
    Thy hasty spring still blasts, and ne'er grows old !

When at Collatium this false lord arrived,   50
Well was he welcom'd by the Roman dame,
Within whose face beauty and virtue strived   †
Which of them both should underprop her fame :
When virtue bragg'd, beauty would blush for shame,
    When beauty boasted blushes, in despite
    Virtue would stain that o'er with silver white.

75

But beauty, in that white entituled,
From Venus' doves doth challenge that fair field :
Then virtue claims from beauty beauty's red,
Which virtue gave the golden age, to gild   60
Their silver cheeks, and call'd it then their shield,
  Teaching them thus to use it in the fight,
  When shame assail'd, the red should fence the white.

This heraldry in Lucrece' face was seen,
Argued by beauty's red and virtue's white :
Of either's colour was the other queen,
Proving from world's minority their right :
Yet their ambition makes them still to fight ;
  The sovereignty of either being so great,
  That oft they interchange each other's seat.   70

This silent war of lilies and of roses,
Which Tarquin view'd in her fair face's field,
In their pure ranks his traitor eye encloses ;
Where, lest between them both it should be kill'd,
The coward captive vanquished doth yield
  To those two armies, that would let him go
  Rather than triumph in so false a foe.

Now thinks he that her husband's shallow tongue,
The niggard prodigal that prais'd her so,
In that high task hath done her beauty wrong,   80
Which far exceeds his barren skill to show :
Therefore that praise which Collatine doth owe
    Enchanted Tarquin answers with surmise,
    In silent wonder of still-gazing eyes.

This earthly saint, adored by this devil,
Little suspecteth the false worshipper ;
For unstain'd thoughts do seldom dream on evil ;
Birds never lim'd no secret bushes fear :
So guiltless she securely gives good cheer
    And reverend welcome to her princely guest,   90
    Whose inward ill no outward harm express'd :

For that he colour'd with his high estate,
Hiding base sin in pleats of majesty ;
That nothing in him seem'd inordinate,
Save sometime too much wonder of his eye,
Which, having all, all could not satisfy ;
    But, poorly rich, so wanteth in his store,
    That, cloy'd with much, he pineth still for more.

But she, that never cop'd with stranger eyes,
Could pick no meaning from their parling looks,   100
Nor read the subtle-shining secrecies,
Writ in the glassy margents of such books :
She touch'd no unknown baits, nor fear'd no hooks,
    Nor could she moralize his wanton sight,
    More than his eyes were open'd to the light.

He stories to her ears her husband's fame,
Won in the fields of fruitful Italy ;
And decks with praises Collatine's high name,
Made glorious by his manly chivalry,
With bruised arms and wreaths of victory :   110
    Her joy with heav'd-up hand she doth express,
    And wordless so greets heaven for his success.

Far from the purpose of his coming thither,
He makes excuses for his being there :
No cloudy show of stormy blustering weather
Doth yet in his fair welkin once appear ;
Till sable Night, mother of dread and fear,   †
    Upon the world dim darkness doth display,
    And in her vaulty prison stows the day.

For then is Tarquin brought unto his bed,   120
Intending weariness with heavy spright;
For after supper long he questioned
With modest Lucrece, and wore out the night:
Now leaden slumber with life's strength doth fight;
    And every one to rest himself betakes,   †
    Save thieves, and cares, and troubled minds that wakes.

As one of which doth Tarquin lie revolving
The sundry dangers of his will's obtaining;
Yet ever to obtain his will resolving,
Though weak-built hopes persuade him to abstaining: 130
Despair to gain doth traffic oft for gaining,
    And when great treasure is the meed proposed,
    Though death be adjunct, there's no death supposed.

Those that much covet are with gain so fond
That what they have not, that which they possess   †
They scatter and unloose it from their bond,
And so, by hoping more, they have but less;
Or, gaining more, the profit of excess
    Is but to surfeit, and such griefs sustain,
    That they prove bankrupt in this poor-rich gain   140

The aim of all is but to nurse the life
With honour, wealth, and ease, in waning age;
And in this aim there is such thwarting strife
That one for all or all for one we gage;
As life for honour in fell battle's rage,
      Honour for wealth, and oft that wealth doth cost
      The death of all, and altogether lost.

So that in venturing ill we leave to be
The things we are for that which we expect;
And this ambitious foul infirmity,   150
In having much, torments us with defect
Of that we have: so then we do neglect
      The thing we have, and, all for want of wit,
      Make something nothing, by augmenting it.

Such hazard now must doting Tarquin make,
Pawning his honour to obtain his lust,
And for himself himself he must forsake:
Then where is truth, if there be no self-trust?
When shall he think to find a stranger just,
      When he himself himself confounds, betrays   160
      To slanderous tongues and wretched hateful days?

Now stole upon the time the dead of night,
When heavy sleep had clos'd up mortal eyes,
No comfortable star did lend his light,
No noise but owls' and wolves' death-boding cries;
Now serves the season that they may surprise
    The silly lambs : pure thoughts are dead and still,
    While lust and murder wakes to stain and kill.

And now this lustful lord leapt from his bed,
Throwing his mantle rudely o'er his arm,   170
Is madly toss'd between desire and dread ;
Th' one sweetly flatters, th' other feareth harm,
But honest fear, bewitch'd with lust's foul charm,
    Doth too too oft betake him to retire,
    Beaten away by brain-sick rude desire.

His falchion on a flint he softly smiteth,
That from the cold stone sparks of fire do fly,
Whereat a waxen torch forthwith he lighteth,
Which must be lode-star to his lustful eye ;
And to the flame thus speaks advisedly :   180
    ' As from this cold flint I enforc'd this fire,
    So Lucrece must I force to my desire.'

81

Here pale with fear he doth premeditate
The dangers of his loathsome enterprise,
And in his inward mind he doth debate
What following sorrow may on this arise :
Then, looking scornfully, he doth despise
      His naked armour of still-slaughter'd lust,
      And justly thus controls his thoughts unjust :

' Fair torch, burn out thy light, and lend it not   190
To darken her whose light excelleth thine :
And die, unhallow'd thoughts, before you blot
With your uncleanness that which is divine :
Offer pure incense to so pure a shrine :
      Let fair humanity abhor the deed
      That spots and stains love's modest snow-white weed.

' O shame to knighthood, and to shining arms !
O foul dishonour to my household's grave !
O impious act, including all foul harms !
A martial man to be soft fancy's slave !   200
True valour still a true respect should have ;
      Then my digression is so vile, so base,
      That it will live engraven in my face.

' Yea, though I die, the scandal will survive,
And be an eye-sore in my golden coat;
Some loathsome dash the herald will contrive,
To cipher me how fondly I did dote;
That my posterity, shamed with the note,
    Shall curse my bones, and hold it for no sin
      To wish that I their father had not been.   210

' What win I, if I gain the thing I seek?
A dream, a breath, a froth of fleeting joy,
Who buys a minute's mirth to wail a week?
Or sells eternity to get a toy?
For one sweet grape who will the vine destroy?
    Or what fond beggar, but to touch the crown,
      Would with the sceptre straight be strucken down?

' If Collatinus dream of my intent,
Will he not wake, and in a desperate rage
Post hither, this vile purpose to prevent?   220
This siege that hath engirt his marriage,
This blur to youth, this sorrow to the sage,
    This dying virtue, this surviving shame,
      Whose crime will bear an ever-during blame.

' O what excuse can my invention make,
When thou shalt charge me with so black a deed ?
Will not my tongue be mute, my frail joints shake,
Mine eyes forgo their light, my false heart bleed ?
The guilt being great, the fear doth still exceed ;
  And extreme fear can neither fight not fly,   230
  But coward-like with trembling terror die.

' Had Collatinus kill'd my son or sire,
Or lain in ambush to betray my life,
Or were he not my dear friend, this desire
Might have excuse to work upon his wife,
As in revenge or quittal of such strife :
  But as he is my kinsman, my dear friend,
  The shame and faults finds no excuse nor end.

' Shameful it is ; ay, if the fact be known :
Hateful it is ; there is no hate in loving :   240
I 'll beg her love ; but she is not her own :
The worst is but denial and reproving :
My will is strong, past reason's weak removing.
  Who fears a sentence or an old man's saw
  Shall by a painted cloth be kept in awe.'

                 †

Thus graceless holds he disputation
'Tween frozen conscience and hot-burning will,
And with good thoughts makes dispensation,
Urging the worser sense for vantage still :
Which in a moment doth confound and kill   250
    All pure effects, and doth so far proceed
    That what is vile shows like a virtuous deed.

Quoth he, ' she took me kindly by the hand,
And gazed for tidings in my eager eyes,
Fearing some hard news from the warlike band,
Where her beloved Collatinus lies.
O, how her fear did make her colour rise !
    First red as roses that on lawn we lay,
    Then white as lawn, the roses took away.

' And how her hand, in my hand being lock'd,   260
Forc'd it to tremble with her loyal fear !
Which struck her sad, and then it faster rock'd,
Until her husband's welfare she did hear ;
Whereat she smiled with so sweet a cheer
    That had Narcissus seen her as she stood
    Self-love had never drown'd him in the flood.

' Why hunt I then for colour or excuses ?
All orators are dumb when beauty pleadeth ;   †
Poor wretches have remorse in poor abuses ;
Love thrives not in the heart that shadows dreadeth :   270
Affection is my captain, and he leadeth ;
    And when his gaudy banner is display'd,
    The coward fights, and will not be dismay'd.

' Then, childish fear avaunt, debating die,
Respect and reason wait on wrinkled age !
My heart shall never countermand mine eye :
Sad pause and deep regard beseems the sage ;
My part is youth, and beats these from the stage :
    Desire my pilot is, beauty my prize,
    Then who fears sinking where such treasure lies ? '   280

As corn o'ergrown by weeds, so heedful fear
Is almost choked by unresisted lust.
Away he steals with open listening ear,
Full of foul hope, and full of fond mistrust ;
Both which, as servitors to the unjust,
    So cross him with their opposite persuasion,
    That now he vows a league, and now invasion.

Within his thought her heavenly image sits,
And in the self-same seat sits Collatine :
That eye which looks on her confounds his wits,   290
That eye which him beholds, as more divine,
Unto a view so false will not incline ;
    But with a pure appeal seeks to the heart,
    Which once corrupted takes the worser part ;

And therein heartens up his servile powers,
Who, flatter'd by their leader's jocund show,
Stuff up his lust, as minutes fill up hours ;
And as their captain, so their pride doth grow,
Paying more slavish tribute than they owe.
    By reprobate desire thus madly led,   300
    The Roman lord marcheth to Lucrece' bed.

The locks between her chamber and his will,
Each one by him enforc'd retires his ward ;
But, as they open, they all rate his ill,
Which drives the creeping thief to some regard :
The threshold grates the door to have him heard ;
    Night-wandering weasels shriek to see him there ;
    They fright him, yet he still pursues his fear.

As each unwilling portal yields him way,
Through little vents and crannies of the place   310
The wind wars with his torch to make him stay,
And blows the smoke of it into his face,
Extinguishing his conduct in this case ;
    But his hot heart, which fond desire doth scorch,
    Puffs forth another wind that fires the torch :

And being lighted, by the light he spies
Lucretia's glove, wherein her needle sticks :
He takes it from the rushes where it lies,
And griping it, the needle his finger pricks ;
As who should say ' This glove to wanton tricks   320
    Is not inur'd ; return again in haste ;
    Thou see'st our mistress' ornaments are chaste.'

But all these poor forbiddings could not stay him ;
He in the worst sense consters their denial :
The doors, the wind, the glove, that did delay him,
He takes for accidental things of trial ;
Or as those bars which stop the hourly dial,
    Who with a lingering stay his course doth let,
    Till every minute pays the hour his debt.

'So, so,' quoth he, 'these lets attend the time,   330
Like little frosts that sometimes threat the spring
To add a more rejoicing to the prime,
And give the sneaped birds more cause to sing.
Pain pays the income of each precious thing ;
  Huge rocks, high winds, strong pirates, shelves and
    sands,
  The merchant fears, ere rich at home he lands.'

Now is he come unto the chamber door,
That shuts him from the heaven of his thought,
Which with a yielding latch, and with no more,
Hath barr'd him from the blessed thing he sought.   340
So from himself impiety hath wrought,
  That for his prey to pray he doth begin,
  As if the heavens should countenance his sin.

But in the midst of his unfruitful prayer,
Having solicited the eternal power
That his foul thoughts might compass his fair fair,
And they would stand auspicious to the hour,
Even there he starts : quoth he, 'I must deflower :
  The powers to whom I pray abhor this fact ;
  How can they then assist me in the act ?   350

' Then Love and Fortune be my gods, my guide !
My will is back'd with resolution :   †
Thoughts are but dreams till their effects be tried ;
The blackest sin is clear'd with absolution ;
Against love's fire fear's frost hath dissolution.
      The eye of heaven is out, and misty night
      Covers the shame that follows sweet delight.'

This said, his guilty hand pluck'd up the latch,
And with his knee the door he opens wide.
The dove sleeps fast that this night-owl will catch :   360
Thus treason works ere traitors be espied.
Who sees the lurking serpent steps aside ;
      But she, sound sleeping, fearing no such thing,
      Lies at the mercy of his mortal sting.

Into the chamber wickedly he stalks,
And gazeth on her yet unstained bed.
The curtains being close, about he walks,
Rolling his greedy eyeballs in his head :
By their high treason is his heart misled,
      Which gives the watch-word to his hand full soon   370
      To draw the cloud that hides the silver moon.

Look, as the fair and fiery-pointed sun,
Rushing from forth a cloud, bereaves our sight ;
Even so, the curtain drawn, his eyes begun
To wink, being blinded with a greater light :
Whether it is that she reflects so bright,
  That dazzleth them, or else some shame supposed,
  But blind they are, and keep themselves enclosed.

O, had they in that darksome prison died !
Then had they seen the period of their ill ;   380
Then Collatine again, by Lucrece' side,
In his clear bed might have reposed still :
But they must ope, this blessed league to kill ;
  And holy-thoughted Lucrece to their sight
  Must sell her joy, her life, her world's delight.

Her lily hand her rosy cheek lies under,
Cozening the pillow of a lawful kiss ;
Who, therefore angry, seems to part in sunder,
Swelling on either side to want his bliss ;
Between whose hills her head entombed is :   390
  Where, like a virtuous monument, she lies,
  To be admir'd of lewd unhallow'd eyes.

91

Without the bed her other fair hand was,
On the green coverlet, whose perfect white
Show'd like an April daisy on the grass,
With pearly sweat, resembling dew of night.
Her eyes, like marigolds, had sheath'd their light,
  And canopied in darkness sweetly lay,
  Till they might open to adorn the day.

Her hair, like golden threads, play'd with her breath ;   400
O modest wantons, wanton modesty !
Showing life's triumph in the map of death,
And death's dim look in life's mortality :
Each in her sleep themselves so beautify
  As if between them twain there were no strife,
  But that life liv'd in death and death in life.

Her breasts, like ivory globes circled with blue,
A pair of maiden worlds unconquered,
Save of their lord, no bearing yoke they knew,
And him by oath they truly honoured.   410
These worlds in Tarquin new ambition bred,
  Who, like a foul usurper, went about
  From this fair throne to heave the owner out.

What could he see but mightily he noted ?
What did he note but strongly he desired ?
What he beheld, on that he firmly doted,
And in his will his wilful eye he tired.
With more than admiration he admired
    Her azure veins, her alabaster skin,
    Her coral lips, her snow-white dimpled chin.   420

As the grim lion fawneth o'er his prey,
Sharp hunger by the conquest satisfied,
So o'er this sleeping soul doth Tarquin stay,
His rage of lust by gazing qualified ;
Slack'd not suppress'd ; for standing by her side,
    His eye, which late this mutiny restrains,
    Unto a greater uproar tempts his veins :

And they, like straggling slaves for pillage fighting,
Obdurate vassals fell exploits effecting,
In bloody death and ravishment delighting,   430
Nor children's tears nor mothers' groans respecting,
Swell in their pride, the onset still expecting :
    Anon his beating heart, alarum striking,
    Gives the hot charge, and bids them do their liking.

His drumming heart cheers up his burning eye,
His eye commends the leading to his hand ;
His hand, as proud of such a dignity,
Smoking with pride, march'd on to make his stand
On her bare breast, the heart of all her land :
      Whose ranks of blue veins, as his hand did scale,   440
      Left their round turrets destitute and pale.

They, mustering to the quiet cabinet
Where their dear governess and lady lies,
Do tell her she is dreadfully beset,
And fright her with confusion of their cries :
She, much amaz'd, breaks ope her lock'd-up eyes,
      Who, peeping forth this tumult to behold,
      Are by his flaming torch dimm'd and controll'd.

Imagine her as one in dead of night
From forth dull sleep by dreadful fancy waking,   450
That thinks she hath beheld some ghastly sprite,
Whose grim aspect sets every joint a-shaking ;
What terror 'tis ! but she, in worser taking,
      From sleep disturbed, heedfully doth view
      The sight which makes supposed terror true.

Wrapp'd and confounded in a thousand fears,
Like to a new-kill'd bird she trembling lies ;
She dares not look ; yet, winking, there appears
Quick-shifting antics, ugly in her eyes :
Such shadows are the weak brain's forgeries :   460
  Who, angry that the eyes fly from their lights,
  In darkness daunts them with more dreadful sights.

His hand, that yet remains upon her breast,
(Rude ram, to batter such an ivory wall !)
May feel her heart, poor citizen ! distress'd,
Wounding itself to death, rise up and fall,
Beating her bulk, that his hand shakes withal.
  This moves in him more rage and lesser pity,
  To make the breach and enter this sweet city.

First, like a trumpet, doth his tongue begin   470
To sound a parley to his heartless foe,
Who o'er the white sheet peers her whiter chin,
The reason of this rash alarm to know,
Which he by dumb demeanour seeks to show
  But she with vehement prayers urgeth still
  Under what colour he commits this ill.

Thus he replies : ' The colour in thy face,
That even for anger makes the lily pale
And the red rose at blush her own disgrace,
Shall plead for me and tell my loving tale :   480
Under that colour am I come to scale
    Thy never-conquer'd fort : the fault is thine,
    For those thine eyes betray thee unto mine.

' Thus I forestall thee, if thou mean to chide :
Thy beauty hath ensnar'd thee to this night,
Where thou with patience must my will abide,
My will that marks thee for my earth's delight,
Which I to conquer sought with all my might ;
    But as reproof and reason beat it dead,
    By thy bright beauty was it newly bred.   490

' I see what crosses my attempt will bring,
I know what thorns the growing rose defends,
I think the honey guarded with a sting,
All this beforehand counsel comprehends :
But will is deaf, and hears no heedful friends ;
    Only he hath an eye to gaze on beauty,
    And dotes on what he looks, 'gainst law or duty.

'I have debated, even in my soul,
What wrong, what shame, what sorrow I shall breed,
But nothing can affection's course control,   500
Or stop the headlong fury of his speed.
I know repentant tears ensue the deed,
    Reproach, disdain, and deadly enmity,
    Yet strive I to embrace mine infamy.'

This said, he shakes aloft his Roman blade,
Which, like a falcon towering in the skies,
Coucheth the fowl below with his wings' shade,
Whose crooked beak threats if he mount he dies:
So under his insulting falchion lies
    Harmless Lucretia, marking what he tells   510
    With trembling fear, as fowl hear falcon's bells.

'Lucrece,' quoth he, 'this night I must enjoy thee:
If thou deny, then force must work my way,
For in thy bed I purpose to destroy thee:
That done, some worthless slave of thine I'll slay,
To kill thine honour with thy life's decay;
    And in thy dead arms do I mean to place him,
    Swearing I slew him, seeing thee embrace him.

97

' So thy surviving husband shall remain
The scornful mark of every open eye ;   520
Thy kinsmen hang their heads at this disdain,
Thy issue blurr'd with nameless bastardy :
And thou, the author of their obloquy
    Shalt have thy trespass cited up in rhymes,
    And sung by children in succeeding times.

' But if thou yield, I rest thy secret friend :
The fault unknown is as a thought unacted ;
A little harm done to a great good end
For lawful policy remains enacted.
The poisonous simple sometime is compacted   530
    In a pure compound ; being so applied,   †
    His venom in effect is purified.

' Then, for thy husband and thy children's sake,
Tender my suit, bequeath not to their lot
The shame that from them no device can take,
The blemish that will never be forgot ;
Worse than a slavish wipe or birth-hour's blot :
    For marks descried in men's nativity
    Are nature's faults, not their own infamy.'

Here with a cockatrice' dead-killing eye   540
He rouseth up himself, and makes a pause,
While she, the picture of pure piety,   †
Like a white hind under the gripe's sharp claws,
Pleads in a wilderness where are no laws
    To the rough beast that knows no gentle right,
    Nor aught obeys but his foul appetite.

But when a black-faced cloud the world doth threat,
In his dim mist the aspiring mountains hiding,
From earth's dark womb some gentle gust doth get,
Which blows these pitchy vapours from their biding,   550
Hindering their present fall by this dividing ;
    So his unhallow'd haste her words delays,
    And moody Pluto winks while Orpheus plays.

Yet, foul night-waking cat, he doth but dally,
While in his hold-fast foot the weak mouse panteth :
Her sad behaviour feeds his vulture folly,
A swallowing gulf that even in plenty wanteth ;
His ear her prayers admits, but his heart granteth
    No penetrable entrance to her plaining :
    Tears harden lust, though marble wear with raining.

Her pity-pleading eyes are sadly fixed   561
In the remorseless wrinkles of his face ;
Her modest eloquence with sighs is mixed,
Which to her oratory adds more grace.
She puts the period often from his place,
    And midst the sentence so her accent breaks
    That twice she doth begin ere once she speaks.

She conjures him by high almighty Jove,
By knighthood, gentry, and sweet friendship's oath,
By her untimely tears, her husband's love,   570
By holy human law and common troth,
By heaven and earth, and all the power of both,
    That to his borrow'd bed he make retire,
    And stoop to honour, not to foul desire.

Quoth she : ' Reward not hospitality
With such black payment as thou hast pretended ;
Mud not the fountain that gave drink to thee,
Mar not the thing that cannot be amended ;
End thy ill aim before thy shoot be ended ;
    He is no woodman that doth bend his bow   580
    To strike a poor unseasonable doe.

'My husband is thy friend, for his sake spare me;
Thyself art mighty, for thine own sake leave me;
Myself a weakling, do not then ensnare me:
Thou look'st not like deceit, do not deceive me.
My sighs like whirlwinds labour hence to heave thee:
    If ever man were mov'd with woman's moans,
    Be moved with my tears, my sighs, my groans:

'All which together, like a troubled ocean,
Beat at thy rocky and wreck-threatening heart,   590
To soften it with their continual motion;
For stones dissolv'd to water do convert.
O, if no harder than a stone thou art,
    Melt at my tears, and be compassionate!
    Soft pity enters at an iron gate.

'In Tarquin's likeness I did entertain thee;
Hast thou put on his shape, to do him shame?
To all the host of heaven I complain me,
Thou wrong'st his honour, wound'st his princely name.
Thou art not what thou seem'st, and if the same,   600
    Thou seem'st not what thou art, a god, a king;
    For kings like gods should govern every thing.

' How will thy shame be seeded in thine age,
When thus thy vices bud before thy spring !
If in thy hope thou dar'st do such outrage,
What dar'st thou not when once thou art a king ?
O, be remember'd, no outrageous thing
    From vassal actors can be wip'd away ;
    Then kings' misdeeds cannot be hid in clay.

' This deed will make thee only lov'd for fear ;   610
But happy monarchs still are fear'd for love :
With foul offenders thou perforce must bear,
When they in thee the like offences prove :
If but for fear of this, thy will remove ;
    For princes are the glass, the school, the book,
    Where subjects' eyes do learn, do read, do look.

' And wilt thou be the school where Lust shall learn ?
Must he in thee read lectures of such shame ?
Wilt thou be glass wherein it shall discern
Authority for sin, warrant for blame,   620
To privilege dishonour in thy name ?
    Thou back'st reproach against long-living laud,
    And mak'st fair reputation but a bawd.

'Hast thou command? by him that gave it thee,
From a pure heart command thy rebel will:
Draw not thy sword to guard iniquity,
For it was lent thee all that brood to kill.
Thy princely office how canst thou fulfil,
　　When, pattern'd by thy fault, foul sin may say
　　He learn'd to sin and thou didst teach the way?　　630

'Think but how vile a spectacle it were,
To view thy present trespass in another.
Men's faults do seldom to themselves appear;
Their own transgressions partially they smother:
This guilt would seem death-worthy in thy brother.
　　O, how are they wrapp'd in with infamies
　　That from their own misdeeds askance their eyes!

'To thee, to thee, my heav'd-up hands appeal,
Not to seducing lust, thy rash relier:
I sue for exil'd majesty's repeal,　　640
Let him return, and flattering thoughts retire:
His true respect will prison false desire,
　　And wipe the dim mist from thy doting eyne,
　　That thou shalt see thy state and pity mine.'

'Have done,' quoth he : 'my uncontrolled tide
Turns not, but swells the higher by this let.
Small lights are soon blown out, huge fires abide,
And with the wind in greater fury fret :
The petty streams that pay a daily debt
    To their salt sovereign, with their fresh falls' haste   650
    Add to his flow, but alter not his taste.'

'Thou art,' quoth she, 'a sea, a sovereign king,
And, lo, there falls into thy boundless flood
Black lust, dishonour, shame, misgoverning,
Who seek to stain the ocean of thy blood.
If all these petty ills shall change thy good,
    Thy sea within a puddle's womb is hearsed,
    And not the puddle in thy sea dispersed.

'So shall these slaves be king, and thou their slave,
Thou nobly base, they basely dignified ;   660
Thou their fair life, and they thy fouler grave,
Thou loathed in their shame, they in thy pride :
The lesser thing should not the greater hide ;
    The cedar stoops not to the base shrub's foot,
    But low shrubs wither at the cedar's root.

'So let thy thoughts, low vassals to thy state'—
'No more,' quoth he ; ' by heaven, I will not hear thee :
Yield to my love ; if not, enforced hate,
Instead of love's coy touch, shall rudely tear thee :
That done, despitefully I mean to bear thee   670
    Unto the base bed of some rascal groom,
    To be thy partner in this shameful doom.'

This said, he sets his foot upon the light,
For light and lust are deadly enemies :
Shame folded up in blind concealing night,
When most unseen, then most doth tyrannize.
The wolf hath seiz'd his prey, the poor lamb cries ;
    Till with her own white fleece her voice controll'd
    Entombs her outcry in her lips' sweet fold :

For with the nightly linen that she wears   680
He pens her piteous clamours in her head,
Cooling his hot face in the chastest tears
That ever modest eyes with sorrow shed.
O, that prone lust should stain so pure a bed !   †
    The spots whereof could weeping purify,
    Her tears should drop on them perpetually.

But she hath lost a dearer thing than life,
And he hath won what he would lose again :
This forced league doth force a further strife ;
This momentary joy breeds months of pain ;　　　　690
This hot desire converts to cold disdain :
　　　　Pure chastity is rifled of her store,
　　　　And lust, the thief, far poorer than before.

Look, as the full-fed hound or gorged hawk,
Unapt for tender smell, or speedy flight,
Make slow pursuit, or altogether balk
The prey wherein by nature they delight,
So surfeit-taking Tarquin fares this night :
　　　　His taste delicious, in digestion souring,
　　　　Devours his will that liv'd by foul devouring.　　700

O, deeper sin than bottomless conceit
Can comprehend in still imagination !
Drunken Desire must vomit his receipt,
Ere he can see his own abomination.
While Lust is in his pride, no exclamation
　　　　Can curb his heat or rein his rash desire,
　　　　Till, like a jade, self-will himself doth tire.

And then with lank and lean discolour'd cheek
With heavy eye, knit brow, and strengthless pace,
Feeble Desire, all recreant, poor and meek,　　　　　710
Like to a bankrupt beggar wails his case :
The flesh being proud, Desire doth fight with Grace,
　　　For there it revels, and when that decays
　　　The guilty rebel for remission prays.

So fares it with this faultful lord of Rome,
Who this accomplishment so hotly chased ;
For now against himself he sounds this doom,
That through the length of times he stands disgraced :
Besides, his soul's fair temple is defaced,
　　　To whose weak ruins muster troops of cares,　　720
　　　To ask the spotted princess how she fares.

She says, her subjects with foul insurrection
Have batter'd down her consecrated wall,
And by their mortal fault brought in subjection
Her immortality, and made her thrall
To living death and pain perpetual :
　　　Which in her prescience she controlled still,
　　　But her foresight could not forestall their will.

107

Even in this thought through the dark night he stealeth,
A captive victor that hath lost in gain, 730
Bearing away the wound that nothing healeth,
The scar that will, despite of cure, remain,
Leaving his spoil perplex'd in greater pain.
    She bears the load of lust he left behind,
    And he the burthen of a guilty mind.

He like a thievish dog creeps sadly thence,
She like a wearied lamb lies panting there,
He scowls, and hates himself for his offence,
She, desperate, with her nails her flesh doth tear ;
He faintly flies, sweating with guilty fear ; 740
    She stays, exclaiming on the direful night ;
    He runs, and chides his vanish'd, loath'd delight.

He thence departs a heavy convertite,
She there remains a hopeless cast-away,
He in his speed looks for the morning light,
She prays she never may behold the day ;
' For day,' quoth she, ' night's 'scapes doth open lay,
    And my true eyes have never practis'd how
    To cloak offences with a cunning brow.

' They think not but that every eye can see 750
The same disgrace which they themselves behold ;
And therefore would they still in darkness be,
To have their unseen sin remain untold ;
For they their guilt with weeping will unfold,
    And grave, like water that doth eat in steel,
    Upon my cheeks what helpless shame I feel.'

Here she exclaims against repose and rest,
And bids her eyes hereafter still be blind.
She wakes her heart by beating on her breast,
And bids it leap from thence, where it may find 760
Some purer chest to close so pure a mind.
    Frantic with grief thus breathes she forth her spite
    Against the unseen secrecy of night :

' O comfort-killing Night, image of hell,
Dim register and notary of shame,
Black stage for tragedies and murders fell,
Vast sin-concealing chaos, nurse of blame,
Blind muffled bawd, dark harbour for defame,
    Grim cave of death, whispering conspirator
    With close-tongu'd treason and the ravisher ! 770

' O hateful, vaporous, and foggy Night !
Since thou art guilty of my cureless crime,
Muster thy mists to meet the eastern light,
Make war against proportion'd course of time ;
Or if thou wilt permit the sun to climb
    His wonted height, yet ere he go to bed,
    Knit poisonous clouds about his golden head.

' With rotten damps ravish the morning air,
Let their exhal'd unwholesome breaths make sick
The life of purity, the supreme fair,   780
Ere he arrive his weary noon-tide prick,
And let thy musty vapours march so thick
    That in their smoky ranks his smother'd light
    May set at noon, and make perpetual night.

' Were Tarquin Night, as he is but Night's child,
The silver-shining queen he would disdain ;
Her twinkling handmaids too, by him defil'd,
Through Night's black bosom should not peep again :
So should I have co-partners in my pain,
    And fellowship in woe doth woe assuage,   790
    As palmers' chat makes short their pilgrimage.

'Where now I have no one to blush with me,
To cross their arms and hang their heads with mine,
To mask their brows and hide their infamy,
But I alone, alone, must sit and pine,
Seasoning the earth with showers of silver brine,
      Mingling my talk with tears, my grief with groans,
      Poor wasting monuments of lasting moans.

'O Night, thou furnace of foul-reeking smoke,
Let not the jealous Day behold that face   800
Which underneath thy black all-hiding-cloak
Immodestly lies martyr'd with disgrace!
Keep still possession of thy gloomy place,
      That all the faults which in thy reign are made
      May likewise be sepulchred in thy shade!

'Make me not object to the tell-tale Day!
The light will show, character'd in my brow,
The story of sweet chastity's decay,
The impious breach of holy wedlock vow:
Yea, the illiterate, that know not how   810
      To cipher what is writ in learned books,
      Will cote my loathsome trespass in my looks.

III

' The nurse to still her child will tell my story,
And fright her crying babe with Tarquin's name ;
The orator to deck his oratory
Will couple my reproach to Tarquin's shame ;
Feast-finding minstrels, tuning my defame,
   Will tie the hearers to attend each line,
   How Tarquin wronged me, I Collatine.

' Let my good name, that senseless reputation,   820
For Collatine's dear love be kept unspotted :
If that he made a theme for disputation,
The branches of another root are rotted,
And undeserv'd reproach to him allotted
   That is as clear from this attaint of mine
   As I, ere this, was pure to Collatine.

' O unseen shame, invisible disgrace,
O unfelt sore, crest-wounding, private scar !
Reproach is stamp'd in Collatinus' face,
And Tarquin's eye may read the mot afar,   830
How he in peace is wounded, not in war.
   Alas, how many bear such shameful blows,
   Which not themselves, but he that gives them knows !

'If, Collatine, thine honour lay in me,
From me by strong assault it is bereft;
My honey lost, and I, a drone-like bee,
Have no perfection of my summer left,
But robb'd and ransack'd by injurious theft:
    In thy weak hive a wandering wasp hath crept,
    And suck'd the honey which thy chaste bee kept.   840

'Yet am I guilty of thy honour's wrack;
Yet for thy honour did I entertain him;
Coming from thee, I could not put him back,
For it had been dishonour to disdain him:
Besides, of weariness he did complain him,
    And talk'd of virtue: O unlooked-for evil,
    When virtue is profan'd in such a devil!

'Why should the worm intrude the maiden bud?
Or hateful cuckoos hatch in sparrows' nests?
Or toads infect fair founts with venom mud?   850
Or tyrant folly lurk in gentle breasts?
Or kings be breakers of their own behests?
    But no perfection is so absolute
    That some impurity doth not pollute.

' The aged man that coffers up his gold
Is plagu'd with cramps, and gouts, and painful fits,
And scarce hath eyes his treasure to behold,
But like still-pining Tantalus he sits,　　　　　　　　†
And useless barns the harvest of his wits ;
　　　Having no other pleasure of his gain　　　　　860
　　　But torment that it cannot cure his pain.

' So then he hath it when he cannot use it,
And leaves it to be master'd by his young ;
Who in their pride do presently abuse it :
Their father was too weak, and they too strong,
To hold their cursed-blessed fortune long.
　　　The sweets we wish for turn to loathed sours,
　　　Even in the moment that we call them ours.

' Unruly blasts wait on the tender spring,
Unwholesome weeds take root with precious flowers,　　870
The adder hisses where the sweet birds sing,
What virtue breeds iniquity devours :
We have no good that we can say is ours
　　　But ill-annexed Opportunity
　　　Or kills his life or else his quality.

' O Opportunity, thy guilt is great !
'Tis thou that execut'st the traitor's treason ;
Thou sets the wolf where he the lamb may get ;
Whoever plots the sin, thou point'st the season ;
'Tis thou that spurn'st at right, at law, at reason ;   880
    And in thy shady cell, where none may spy him,
    Sits Sin to seize the souls that wander by him.

' Thou makest the vestal violate her oath,
Thou blow'st the fire when temperance is thaw'd,
Thou smother'st honesty, thou murdrest troth,
Thou foul abettor, thou notorious bawd !
Thou plantest scandal, and displacest laud :
    Thou ravisher, thou traitor, thou false thief,
    Thy honey turns to gall, thy joy to grief !

' Thy secret pleasure turns to open shame,   890
Thy private feasting to a public fast,
Thy smoothing titles to a ragged name,
Thy sugar'd tongue to bitter wormwood taste :
Thy violent vanities can never last.
    How comes it then, vile Opportunity,
    Being so bad, such numbers seek for thee ?

' When wilt thou be the humble suppliant's friend,
And bring him where his suit may be obtained ?
When wilt thou sort an hour great strifes to end ?
Or free that soul which wretchedness hath chained ?   900
Give physic to the sick, ease to the pained ?
> The poor, lame, blind, halt, creep, cry out for thee,
> But they ne'er meet with Opportunity.

' The patient dies while the physician sleeps,
The orphan pines while the oppressor feeds,
Justice is feasting while the widow weeps,
Advice is sporting while infection breeds :
Thou grant'st no time for charitable deeds :
> Wrath, envy, treason, rape, and murder's rages,
> Thy heinous hours wait on them as their pages.   910

' When Truth and Virtue have to do with thee,
A thousand crosses keep them from thy aid :
They buy thy help, but Sin ne'er gives a fee,
He gratis comes, and thou art well appaid
As well to hear as grant what he hath said.
> My Collatine would else have come to me
> When Tarquin did, but he was stay'd by thee.

' Guilty thou art of murder, and of theft,
Guilty of perjury, and subornation,
Guilty of treason, forgery, and shift,   920
Guilty of incest, that abomination ;
An accessary by thine inclination
  To all sins past and all that are to come,
  From the creation to the general doom.

' Mis-shapen Time, copesmate of ugly Night,
Swift subtle post, carrier of grisly care,
Eater of youth, false slave to false delight,
Base watch of woes, sin's pack-horse, virtue's snare !
Thou nursest all and murdrest all that are :
  O hear me then, injurious, shifting Time !   930
  Be guilty of my death, since of my crime.

' Why hath thy servant Opportunity
Betray'd the hours thou gav'st me to repose,
Cancell'd my fortunes, and enchained me
To endless date of never-ending woes ?
Time's office is to fine the hate of foes,
  To eat up errors by opinion bred,
  Not spend the dowry of a lawful bed.

117

'Time's glory is to calm contending kings,
To unmask falsehood, and bring truth to light, 940
To stamp the seal of time in aged things,
To wake the morn, and sentinel the night,
To wrong the wronger till he render right,
 To ruinate proud buildings with thy hours
 And smear with dust their glittering golden towers;

'To fill with worm-holes stately monuments,
To feed oblivion with decay of things,
To blot old books, and alter their contents,
To pluck the quills from ancient ravens' wings,
To dry the old oak's sap, and cherish springs, †
 To spoil antiquities of hammer'd steel, 951
 And turn the giddy round of Fortune's wheel;

'To show the beldam daughters of her daughter,
To make the child a man, the man a child,
To slay the tiger that doth live by slaughter,
To tame the unicorn and lion wild,
To mock the subtle in themselves beguil'd,
 To cheer the ploughman with increaseful crops,
 And waste huge stones with little water-drops.

' Why work'st thou mischief in thy pilgrimage,   960
Unless thou couldst return to make amends ?
One poor retiring minute in an age
Would purchase thee a thousand thousand friends,
Lending him wit that to bad debtors lends :
    O, this dread night, wouldst thou one hour come back,
    I could prevent this storm, and shun thy wrack !

' Thou ceaseless lackey to eternity,
With some mischance cross Tarquin in his flight:
Devise extremes beyond extremity,
To make him curse this cursed crimeful night :   970
Let ghastly shadows his lewd eyes affright,
    And the dire thought of his committed evil
    Shape every bush a hideous shapeless devil.

' Disturb his hours of rest with restless trances,
Afflict him in his bed with bedrid groans,
Let there bechance him pitiful mischances,
To make him moan, but pity not his moans :
Stone him with harden'd hearts, harder than stones,
    And let mild women to him lose their mildness,
    Wilder to him than tigers in their wildness.   980

' Let him have time to tear his curled hair,
Let him have time against himself to rave,
Let him have time of time's help to despair,
Let him have time to live a loathed slave,
Let him have time a beggar's orts to crave,
      And time to see one that by alms doth live
      Disdain to him disdained scraps to give.

' Let him have time to see his friends his foes,
And merry fools to mock at him resort ;
Let him have time to mark how slow time goes   990
In time of sorrow, and how swift and short
His time of folly and his time of sport ;
      And ever let his unrecalling crime
      Have time to wail the abusing of his time.

' O Time, thou tutor both to good and bad,
Teach me to curse him that thou taught'st this ill !
At this own shadow let the thief run mad,
Himself himself seek every hour to kill !
Such wretched hands such wretched blood should spill ;
      For who so base would such an office have   1000
      As slanderous deathsman to so base a slave ?

' The baser is he, coming from a king,
To shame his hope with deeds degenerate ;
The mightier man, the mightier is the thing
That makes him honour'd, or begets him hate ;
For greatest scandal waits on greatest state.
    The moon being clouded presently is miss'd,
    But little stars may hide them when they list.

' The crow may bathe his coal-black wings in mire,
And unperceiv'd fly with the filth away ;   1010
But if the like the snow-white swan desire,
The stain upon his silver down will stay.
Poor grooms are sightless night, kings glorious day :
    Gnats are unnoted wheresoe'er they fly,
    But eagles gaz'd upon with every eye.

' Out, idle words, servants to shallow fools,
Unprofitable sounds, weak arbitrators !
Busy yourselves in skill-contending schools,
Debate where leisure serves with dull debaters ;
To trembling clients be you mediators :   †
    For me, I force not argument a straw,   1020
    Since that my case is past the help of law.

' In vain I rail at Opportunity,
At Time, at Tarquin, and uncheerful Night,
In vain I cavil with mine infamy,
In vain I spurn at my confirm'd despite ;
This helpless smoke of words doth me no right.
      The remedy indeed to do me good
      Is to let forth my foul defiled blood.

' Poor hand, why quiver'st thou at this decree ?   1030
Honour thyself to rid me of this shame,
For if I die, my honour lives in thee,
But if I live, thou liv'st in my defame :
Since thou couldst not defend thy loyal dame,
      And wast afeard to scratch her wicked foe,
      Kill both thyself, and her for yielding so.'

This said, from her be-tumbled couch she starteth,
To find some desperate instrument of death,
But this no slaughterhouse no tool imparteth,
To make more vent for passage of her breath,   1040
Which, thronging through her lips, so vanisheth
      As smoke from Ætna, that in air consumes,
      Or that which from discharged cannon fumes.

'In vain,' quoth she, 'I live, and seek in vain
Some happy mean to end a hapless life.
I feared by Tarquin's falchion to be slain,
Yet for the self-same purpose seek a knife :
But when I fear'd I was a loyal wife :
    So am I now : O no, that cannot be ;
    Of that true type hath Tarquin rifled me.   1050

'O, that is gone for which I sought to live,
And therefore now I need not fear to die ;
To clear this spot by death, at least I give
A badge of fame to slander's livery,
A dying life to living infamy :
    Poor helpless help, the treasure stol'n away,
    To burn the guiltless casket where it lay !

'Well, well, dear Collatine, thou shalt not know
The stained taste of violated troth ;
I will not wrong thy true affection so,   1060
To flatter thee with an infringed oath ;
This bastard graff shall never come to growth ;
    He shall not boast who did thy stock pollute
    That thou art doting father of his fruit.

' Nor shall he smile at thee in secret thought,
Nor laugh with his companions at thy state,
But thou shalt know thy int'rest was not bought
Basely with gold, but stol'n from forth thy gate.
For me, I am the mistress of my fate,
    And with my trespass never will dispense,   1070
    Till life to death acquit my forc'd offence.

' I will not poison thee with my attaint,
Nor fold my fault in cleanly-coin'd excuses ;
My sable ground of sin I will not paint,
To hide the truth of this false night's abuses :
My tongue shall utter all ; mine eyes, like sluices,
    As from a mountain-spring that feeds a dale,
    Shall gush pure streams to purge my impure tale.'

By this, lamenting Philomel had ended
The well-tun'd warble of her nightly sorrow,   1080
And solemn night with slow sad gait descended
To ugly hell, when lo, the blushing morrow
Lends light to all fair eyes that light will borrow :
    But cloudy Lucrece shames herself to see,
    And therefore still in night would cloister'd be.

Revealing day through every cranny spies,
And seems to point her out where she sits weeping ;
To whom she sobbing speaks : ' O eye of eyes,
Why pry'st thou through my window ? leave thy peeping,
Mock with thy tickling beams eyes that are sleeping ;   1090
    Brand not my forehead with thy piercing light,
    For day hath nought to do what's done by night.'

Thus cavils she with every thing she sees ;
True grief is fond and testy as a child,
Who wayward once, his mood with nought agrees :
Old woes, not infant sorrows, bear them mild ;
Continuance tames the one ; the other wild,
    Like an unpractis'd swimmer plunging still
    With too much labour drowns for want of skill.

So she, deep-drenched in a sea of care,   1100
Holds disputation with each thing she views,
And to herself all sorrow doth compare ;
No object but her passion's strength renews,
And as one shifts, another straight ensues :
    Sometime her grief is dumb and hath no words,
    Sometime 'tis mad and too much talk affords.

The little birds that tune their morning's joy
Make her moans mad, with their sweet melody,
For mirth doth search the bottom of annoy,
Sad souls are slain in merry company,   1110
Grief best is pleased with grief's society;
  True sorrow then is feelingly suffic'd
  When with like semblance it is sympathiz'd.

'Tis double death to drown in ken of shore,
He ten times pines, that pines beholding food,
To see the salve doth make the wound ache more;
Great grief grieves most at that would do it good;
Deep woes roll forward like a gentle flood,
  Who, being stopp'd, the bounding banks o'erflows;
  Grief dallied with nor law nor limit knows. 1120

'You mocking birds,' quoth she, 'your tunes entomb
Within your hollow swelling feather'd breasts,
And in my hearing be you mute and dumb,   †
My restless discord loves no stops nor rests;
A woeful hostess brooks not merry guests:
  Relish your nimble notes to pleasing ears;
  Distress likes dumps when time is kept with tears.

' Come, Philomel, that sing'st of ravishment,   †
Make thy sad grove in my dishevell'd hair :
As the dank earth weeps at thy languishment,   1130
So I at each sad strain will strain a tear,
And with deep groans the diapason bear ;
    For burden-wise I 'll hum on Tarquin still,
    While thou on Tereus descants better skill.   †

' And whiles against a thorn thou bear'st thy part,
To keep thy sharp woes waking, wretched I,
To imitate thee well, against my heart
Will fix a sharp knife, to affright mine eye,
Who, if it wink, shall thereon fall and die.
    These means, as frets upon an instrument,   1140
    Shall tune our heart-strings to true languishment.

' And for, poor bird, thou sing'st not in the day,
As shaming any eye should thee behold,
Some dark deep desert, seated from the way,
That knows not parching heat, nor freezing cold,
Will we find out ; and there we will unfold
    To creatures stern, sad tunes to change their kinds,
    Since men prove beasts, let beasts bear gentle minds.'

As the poor frighted deer, that stands at gaze,
Wildly determining which way to fly,   1150
Or one encompass'd with a winding maze,
That cannot tread the way out readily ;
So with herself is she in mutiny,
    To live or die, which of the twain were better,
    When life is sham'd and death reproach's debtor.   †

' To kill myself,' quoth she, ' alack, what were it,
But with my body my poor soul's pollution ?
They that lose half with greater patience bear it
Than they whose whole is swallow'd in confusion.
That mother tries a merciless conclusion   1160
    Who, having two sweet babes, when death takes one,
    Will slay the other, and be nurse to none.

' My body or my soul, which was the dearer,
When the one pure, the other made divine ?
Whose love of either to myself was nearer,
When both were kept for heaven and Collatine ?
Ay me ! the bark pill'd from the lofty pine,
    His leaves will wither, and his sap decay ;
    So must my soul, her bark being pill'd away.

'Her house is sack'd, her quiet interrupted,   1170
Her mansion batter'd by the enemy,
Her sacred temple spotted, spoil'd, corrupted,
Grossly engirt with daring infamy :
Then let it not be call'd impiety,
        If in this blemish'd fort I make some hole,
        Through which I may convey this troubled soul.

'Yet die I will not, till my Collatine
Have heard the cause of my untimely death,
That he may vow, in that sad hour of mine,
Revenge on him that made me stop my breath ;   1180
My stained blood to Tarquin I'll bequeath,
        Which by him tainted shall for him be spent,
        And as his due writ in my testament.

'My honour I'll bequeath unto the knife
That wounds my body so dishonoured.
'Tis honour to deprive dishonour'd life ;
The one will live, the other being dead :
So of shame's ashes shall my fame be bred,
        For in my death I murder shameful scorn,
        My shame so dead, mine honour is new-born.   1190

' Dear lord of that dear jewel I have lost,
What legacy shall I bequeath to thee ?
My resolution, love, shall be thy boast,
By whose example thou reveng'd mayst be.
How Tarquin must be us'd, read it in me ;
    Myself, thy friend, will kill myself, thy foe,
    And, for my sake, serve thou false Tarquin so.

' This brief abridgement of my will I make :
My soul and body to the skies and ground ;
My resolution, husband, do thou take,   1200
Mine honour be the knife's that makes my wound,
My shame be his that did my fame confound ;
    And all my fame that lives disbursed be
    To those that live and think no shame of me.

' Thou, Collatine, shalt oversee this will ;
How was I overseen that thou shalt see it !
My blood shall wash the slander of mine ill,
My life's foul deed, my life's fair end shall free it.
Faint not, faint heart, but stoutly say " So be it : "
    Yield to my hand, my hand shall conquer thee,   1210
    Thou dead, both die, and both shall victors be.'

This plot of death when sadly she had laid,
And wip'd the brinish pearl from her bright eyes,
With untun'd tongue she hoarsely calls her maid,
Whose swift obedience to her mistress hies;
For fleet-wing'd duty with thought's feathers flies.
  Poor Lucrece' cheeks unto her maid seem so
  As winter meads when sun doth melt their snow.

Her mistress she doth give demure good-morrow,
With soft slow tongue, true mark of modesty,   1220
And sorts a sad look to her lady's sorrow,
For why her face wore sorrow's livery,
But durst not ask of her audaciously
  Why her two suns were cloud-eclipsed so,
  Nor why her fair cheeks over-wash'd with woe.

But as the earth doth weep, the sun being set,
Each flower moisten'd like a melting eye,
Even so the maid with swelling drops 'gan wet
Her circled eyne, enforc'd by sympathy
Of those fair suns set in her mistress' sky,   1230
  Who in a salt-wav'd ocean quench their light,
  Which makes the maid weep like the dewy night.

A pretty while these pretty creatures stand,
Like ivory conduits coral cisterns filling :
One justly weeps, the other takes in hand
No cause, but company, of her drops spilling :
Their gentle sex to weep are often willing,
  Grieving themselves to guess at others' smarts,
  And then they drown their eyes, or break their hearts.

For men have marble, women waxen, minds, 1240
And therefore are they form'd as marble will ;
The weak oppress'd, the impression of strange kinds
Is form'd in them by force, by fraud, or skill :
Then call them not the authors of their ill,
  No more than wax shall be accounted evil
  Wherein is stamp'd the semblance of a devil.

Their smoothness, like a goodly champaign plain,
Lays open all the little worms that creep ;
In men, as in a rough-grown grove, remain
Cave-keeping evils that obscurely sleep : 1250
Through crystal walls each little mote will peep :
  Though men can cover crimes with bold stern looks,
  Poor women's faces are their own faults' books.

No man inveigh against the withered flower,
But chide rough winter that the flower hath kill'd :
Not that devour'd, but that which doth devour,
Is worthy blame ; O, let it not be hild
Poor women's faults, that they are so fulfill'd
    With men's abuses : those proud lords to blame
    Make weak-made women tenants to their shame.   1260

The precedent whereof in Lucrece view,
Assail'd by night with circumstances strong
Of present death, and shame that might ensue
By that her death, to do her husband wrong :
Such danger to resistance did belong
    That dying fear through all her body spread ;
    And who cannot abuse a body dead ?

By this, mild patience bid fair Lucrece speak
To the poor counterfeit of her complaining :
' My girl,' quoth she, ' on what occasion break   1270
Those tears from thee, that down thy cheeks are raining ?
If thou dost weep for grief of my sustaining,
    Know, gentle wench, it small avails my mood :
    If tears could help, mine own would do me good.

' But tell me, girl, when went '—and there she stay'd
Till after a deep groan—' Tarquin from hence ? '
' Madam, ere I was up,' replied the maid,
' The more to blame my sluggard negligence :
Yet with the fault I thus far can dispense ;
    Myself was stirring ere the break of day,   1280
    And ere I rose was Tarquin gone away.

' But, lady, if your maid may be so bold,
She would request to know your heaviness.'
' O, peace ! ' quoth Lucrece : ' if it should be told,
The repetition cannot make it less,
For more it is than I can well express,
    And that deep torture may be call'd a hell
    When more is felt than one hath power to tell.

' Go, get me hither paper, ink, and pen :
Yet save that labour, for I have them here.   1290
What should I say ?   One of my husband's men
Bid thou be ready, by and by, to bear
A letter to my lord, my love, my dear,
    Bid him with speed prepare to carry it,
    The cause craves haste, and it will soon be writ.'

Her maid is gone, and she prepares to write,
First hovering o'er the paper with her quill :
Conceit and grief an eager combat fight ;
What wit sets down is blotted straight with will ;
This is too curious-good, this blunt and ill :   1300
    Much like a press of people at the door,
    Throng her inventions, which shall go before.

At last she thus begins : ' Thou worthy lord
Of that unworthy wife that greeteth thee,
Health to thy person ! next vouchsafe t' afford—
If ever, love, thy Lucrece thou wilt see—
Some present speed, to come and visit me :
    So, I commend me from our house in grief :
    My woes are tedious, though my words are brief.'

Here folds she up the tenor of her woe,   1310
Her certain sorrow writ uncertainly.
By this short schedule Collatine may know
Her grief, but not her grief's true quality :
She dares not thereof make discovery,
    Lest he should hold it her own gross abuse,
    Ere she with blood had stain'd her stain'd excuse.

Besides, the life and feeling of her passion
She hoards, to spend when he is by to hear her,
When sighs, and groans, and tears may grace the fashion,
Of her disgrace, the better so to clear her   1320
From that suspicion which the world might bear her.
     To shun this blot, she would not blot the letter
     With words, till action might become them better.

To see sad sights moves more than hear them told ;
For then the eye interprets to the ear
The heavy motion that it doth behold,
When every part a part of woe doth bear.
'Tis but a part of sorrow that we hear :
     Deep sounds make lesser noise than shallow fords,
     And sorrow ebbs, being blown with wind of words.

Her letter now is seal'd and on it writ   1331
' At Ardea to my lord with more than haste.'
The post attends, and she delivers it,
Charging the sour-fac'd groom to hie as fast
As lagging fowls before the northern blast :
     Speed more than speed but dull and slow she deems ;
     Extremity still urgeth such extremes.

The homely villain court'sies to her low,
And blushing on her, with a steadfast eye
Receives the scroll without or yea or no,   1340
And forth with bashful innocence doth hie.
But they whose guilt within their bosoms lie
    Imagine every eye beholds their blame,
    For Lucrece thought he blush'd to see her shame :

When, silly groom ! God wot, it was defect
Of spirit, life, and bold audacity ;
Such harmless creatures have a true respect
To talk in deeds, while others saucily
Promise more speed but do it leisurely :
    Even so this pattern of the worn-out age   1350
    Pawn'd honest looks, but laid no words to gage.

His kindled duty kindled her mistrust,
That two red fires in both their faces blazed ;
She thought he blush'd, as knowing Tarquin's lust,
And blushing with him, wistly on him gazed,
Her earnest eye did make him more amazed :
    The more she saw the blood his cheeks replenish,
    The more she thought he spied in her some blemish.

But long she thinks till he return again,
And yet the duteous vassal scarce is gone,　　　　1360
The weary time she cannot entertain,
For now 'tis stale to sigh, to weep, and groan ;
So woe hath wearied woe, moan tired moan,
　　　That she her plaints a little while doth stay,
　　　Pausing for means to mourn some newer way.

At last she calls to mind where hangs a piece
Of skilful painting, made for Priam's Troy,
Before the which is drawn the power of Greece,
For Helen's rape the city to destroy,
Threatening cloud-kissing Ilion with annoy,　　　　1370
　　　Which the conceited painter drew so proud,
　　　As heaven, it seem'd, to kiss the turrets bow'd.

A thousand lamentable objects there,
In scorn of nature, art gave lifeless life ;
Many a dry drop seem'd a weeping tear,
Shed for the slaughter'd husband by the wife ;
The red blood reek'd to show the painter's strife,
　　　And dying eyes gleam'd forth their ashy lights,
　　　Like dying coals burnt out in tedious nights.

There might you see the labouring pioner   1380
Begrim'd with sweat, and smeared all with dust,
And from the towers of Troy there would appear
The very eyes of men through loop-holes thrust,
Gazing upon the Greeks with little lust:
    Such sweet observance in this work was had,
    That one might see those far-off eyes look sad.

In great commanders grace and majesty
You might behold, triumphing in their faces,
In youth, quick bearing and dexterity;
And here and there the painter interlaces   1390
Pale cowards, marching on with trembling paces;
    Which heartless peasants did so well resemble,
    That one would swear he saw them quake and tremble.

In Ajax and Ulysses, O, what art
Of physiognomy might one behold!
The face of either cipher'd either's heart;
Their face their manners most expressly told:
In Ajax's eyes blunt rage and rigour roll'd,
    But the mild glance that sly Ulysses lent
    Show'd deep regard and smiling government.   1400

There pleading might you see grave Nestor stand,
As 'twere encouraging the Greeks to fight,
Making such sober action with his hand
That it beguil'd attention, charm'd the sight:
In speech it seem'd his beard, all silver white,
    Wagg'd up and down, and from his lips did fly
    Thin winding breath which purl'd up to the sky.

About him were a press of gaping faces,
Which seem'd to swallow up his sound advice,
All jointly listening, but with several graces,   1410
As if some mermaid did their ears entice,
Some high, some low, the painter was so nice;
    The scalps of many, almost hid behind,
    To jump up higher seem'd, to mock the mind.

Here one man's hand lean'd on another's head,
His nose being shadow'd by his neighbour's ear,
Here one being throng'd bears back, all boll'n and red,
Another smother'd seems to pelt and swear,
And in their rage such signs of rage they bear
    As, but for loss of Nestor's golden words,   1420
    It seem'd they would debate with angry swords.

For much imaginary work was there,
Conceit deceitful, so compact, so kind,
That for Achilles' image stood his spear
Grip'd in an armed hand ; himself behind
Was left unseen, save to the eye of mind :
    A hand, a foot, a face, a leg, a head,
    Stood for the whole to be imagined.

And from the walls of strong-besieged Troy
When their brave hope, bold Hector, march'd to field,   1430
Stood many Trojan mothers sharing joy
To see their youthful sons bright weapons wield,
And to their hope they such odd action yield,
    That through their light joy seemed to appear,
    Like bright things stain'd, a kind of heavy fear.

And from the strand of Dardan, where they fought,
To Simois' reedy banks the red blood ran,
Whose waves to imitate the battle sought
With swelling ridges, and their ranks began
To break upon the galled shore, and than   1440
    Retire again, till meeting greater ranks
    They join, and shoot their foam at Simois' banks.

To this well-painted piece is Lucrece come,
To find a face where all distress is stell'd.
Many she sees where cares have carved some,
But none where all distress and dolour dwell'd,
Till she despairing Hecuba beheld,
　　Staring on Priam's wounds with her old eyes,
　　Which bleeding under Pyrrhus' proud foot lies.

In her the painter had anatomiz'd　　　　　　1450
Time's ruin, beauty's wreck, and grim care's reign :
Her cheeks with chaps and wrinkles were disguis'd ;
Of what she was no semblance did remain :
Her blue blood chang'd to black in every vein,
　　Wanting the spring that those shrunk pipes had fed,
　　Show'd life imprison'd in a body dead.

On this sad shadow Lucrece spends her eyes,
And shapes her sorrow to the beldam's woes,
Who nothing wants to answer her but cries,
And bitter words to ban her cruel foes :　　　　1460
The painter was no god to lend her those,
　　And therefore Lucrece swears he did her wrong,
　　To give her so much grief and not a tongue.

'Poor instrument,' quoth she, 'without a sound,
I'll tune thy woes with my lamenting tongue,
And drop sweet balm in Priam's painted wound,
And rail on Pyrrhus that hath done him wrong,
And with my tears quench Troy that burns so long,
  And with my knife scratch out the angry eyes
  Of all the Greeks that are thine enemies.   1470

'Show me the strumpet that began this stir,
That with my nails her beauty I may tear:
Thy heat of lust, fond Paris, did incur
This load of wrath, that burning Troy doth bear;
Thy eye kindled the fire that burneth here,
  And here in Troy, for trespass of thine eye,
  The sire, the son, the dame and daughter die.

'Why should the private pleasure of some one
Become the public plague of many moe?
Let sin, alone committed, light alone   1480
Upon his head that hath transgressed so;
Let guiltless souls be freed from guilty woe:
  For one's offence why should so many fall,
  To plague a private sin in general?

' Lo, here weeps Hecuba, here Priam dies,
Here manly Hector faints, here Troilus sounds ;
Here friend by friend in bloody channel lies,
And friend to friend gives unadvised wounds,
And one man's lust these many lives confounds :
  Had doting Priam check'd his son's desire,   1490
  Troy had been bright with fame, and not with fire.'

Here feelingly she weeps Troy's painted woes :
For sorrow, like a heavy-hanging bell,
Once set on ringing, with his own weight goes,
Then little strength rings out the doleful knell ;
So Lucrece, set a-work, sad tales doth tell
  To pencill'd pensiveness, and colour'd sorrow,
  She lends them words, and she their looks doth borrow.

She throws her eyes about the painting round,
And who she finds forlorn she doth lament :   1500
At last she sees a wretched image bound,
That piteous looks to Phrygian shepherds lent :
His face, though full of cares, yet show'd content ;
  Onward to Troy with the blunt swains he goes,
  So mild that patience seem'd to scorn his woes.

In him the painter labour'd with his skill
To hide deceit, and give the harmless show
An humble gait, calm looks, eyes wailing still,
A brow unbent, that seem'd to welcome woe;
Cheeks neither red nor pale, but mingled so   1510
    That blushing red no guilty instance gave,
    Nor ashy pale the fear that false hearts have.

But, like a constant and confirmed devil,
He entertain'd a show so seeming just,
And therein so ensconc'd his secret evil,
That jealousy itself could not mistrust
False-creeping craft and perjury should thrust
    Into so bright a day such black-fac'd storms,
    Or blot with hell-born sin such saint-like forms.

The well-skill'd workman this mild image drew   1520
For perjur'd Sinon, whose enchanting story   †
The credulous old Priam after slew;
Whose words, like wildfire, burnt the shining glory
Of rich-built Ilion, that the skies were sorry,
    And little stars shot from their fixed places,
    When their glass fell wherein they view'd their faces.

This picture she advisedly perus'd,
And chid the painter for his wondrous skill,
Saying, some shape in Sinon's was abus'd ;
So fair a form lodg'd not a mind so ill ;   1530
And still on him she gaz'd, and gazing still
  Such signs of truth in his plain face she spied,
  That she concludes the picture was belied.

' It cannot be,' quoth she, ' that so much guile '—
She would have said ' can lurk in such a look ; '
But Tarquin's shape came in her mind the while,
And from her tongue ' can lurk ' from ' cannot ' took :
' It cannot be ' she in that sense forsook,
  And turn'd it thus, ' It cannot be, I find,
  But such a face should bear a wicked mind :   1540

' For even as subtle Sinon here is painted,
So sober-sad, so weary, and so mild,
As if with grief or travail he had fainted,
To me came Tarquin armed to beguild   †
With outward honesty, but yet defil'd
  With inward vice : as Priam him did cherish,
  So did I Tarquin ; so my Troy did perish.

'Look, look, how listening Priam wets his eyes,
To see those borrow'd tears that Sinon sheds !
Priam, why art thou old, and yet not wise ?　　　1550
For every tear he falls a Trojan bleeds :
His eye drops fire, no water thence proceeds ;
　　　Those round clear pearls of his that move thy pity
　　　Are balls of quenchless fire to burn thy city.

'Such devils steal effects from lightless hell ;
For Sinon in his fire doth quake with cold,
And in that cold hot-burning fire doth dwell ;
These contraries such unity do hold,
Only to flatter fools and make them bold :
　　　So Priam's trust false Sinon's tears doth flatter,　　1560
　　　That he finds means to burn his Troy with water.'

Here, all enrag'd, such passion her assails,
That patience is quite beaten from her breast.
She tears the senseless Sinon with her nails,
Comparing him to that unhappy guest
Whose deed hath made herself herself detest :
　　　At last she smilingly with this gives o'er ;
　　　'Fool, fool !' quoth she, ' his wounds will not be sore.'

Thus ebbs and flows the current of her sorrow,
And time doth weary time with her complaining ;　　　1570
She looks for night, and then she longs for morrow,
And both she thinks too long with her remaining :
Short time seems long in sorrow's sharp sustaining ;
　　　Though woe be heavy, yet it seldom sleeps,
　　　And they that watch see time how slow it creeps.

Which all this time hath overslipp'd her thought,
That she with painted images hath spent,
Being from the feeling of her own grief brought
By deep surmise of others' detriment,
Losing her woes in shows of discontent.　　　1580
　　　It easeth some, though none it ever cured,
　　　To think their dolour others have endured.

But now the mindful messenger come back
Brings home his lord and other company ;
Who finds his Lucrece clad in mourning black :
And round about her tear-distained eye
Blue circles stream'd, like rainbows in the sky :
　　　These water-galls in her dim element
　　　Foretell new storms to those already spent.

Which when her sad-beholding husband saw,   1590
Amazedly in her sad face he stares :
Her eyes, though sod in tears, look'd red and raw,
Her lively colour kill'd with deadly cares ;
He hath no power to ask her how she fares ;
    Both stood, like old acquaintance in a trance,
    Met far from home, wondering each other's chance.

At last he takes her by the bloodless hand,
And thus begins : ' What uncouth ill event
Hath thee befall'n, that thou dost trembling stand ?
Sweet love, what spite hath thy fair colour spent ?   1600
Why art thou thus attir'd in discontent ?
    Unmask, dear dear, this moody heaviness,
    And tell thy grief, that we may give redress.'

Three times with sighs she gives her sorrow fire,
Ere once she can discharge one word of woe :
At length address'd to answer his desire,
She modestly prepares to let them know
Her honour is ta'en prisoner by the foe ;
    While Collatine and his consorted lords
    With sad attention long to hear her words.   1610

And now this pale swan in her watery nest
Begins the sad dirge of her certain ending :
' Few words,' quoth she, ' shall fit the trespass best,
Where no excuse can give the fault amending :
In me moe woes than words are now depending ;
  And my laments would be drawn out too long,
  To tell them all with one poor tired tongue.

' Then be this all the task it hath to say :
Dear husband, in the interest of thy bed
A stranger came, and on that pillow lay   1620
Where thou wast wont to rest thy weary head ;
And what wrong else may be imagined
  By foul enforcement might be done to me,
  From that, alas, thy Lucrece is not free.

' For in the dreadful dead of dark midnight,
With shining falchion in my chamber came
A creeping creature, with a flaming light,
And softly cried " Awake, thou Roman dame,
And entertain my love, else lasting shame
  On thee and thine this night I will inflict,   1630
  If thou my love's desire do contradict.

' " For some hard-favour'd groom of thine," quoth he,
" Unless thou yoke thy liking to my will,
I 'll murder straight, and then I 'll slaughter thee,
And swear I found you where you did fulfil
The loathsome act of lust, and so did kill
     The lechers in their deed ; this act will be
     My fame, and thy perpetual infamy."

' With this, I did begin to start and cry ;
And then against my heart he set his sword,   1640
Swearing, unless I took all patiently,
I should not live to speak another word ;
So should my shame still rest upon record,
     And never be forgot in mighty Rome
     The adulterate death of Lucrece, and her groom.

' Mine enemy was strong, my poor self weak,
(And far the weaker with so strong a fear :)
My bloody judge forbade my tongue to speak,
No rightful plea might plead for justice there :
His scarlet lust came evidence to swear   1650
     That my poor beauty had purloin'd his eyes,
     And when the judge is robb'd, the prisoner dies.

' O teach me how to make mine own excuse !
Or, at the least, this refuge let me find ;
Though my gross blood be stain'd with this abuse,
Immaculate and spotless is my mind ;
That was not forc'd ; that never was inclin'd
    To accessary yieldings, but still pure
    Doth in her poison'd closet yet endure.'

Lo, here, the hopeless merchant of this loss,   1660
With head declin'd, and voice damm'd up with woe,
With sad-set eyes and wretched arms across,
From lips new-waxen pale begins to blow
The grief away that stops his answer so :
    But, wretched as he is, he strives in vain,
    What he breathes out his breath drinks up again.

As through an arch the violent roaring tide
Outruns the eye that doth behold his haste,
Yet in the eddy boundeth in his pride
Back to the strait that forc'd him on so fast,   1670
In rage sent out, recall'd in rage being past :
    Even so his sighs, his sorrows, make a saw,
    To push grief on, and back the same grief draw.

Which speechless woe of his poor she attendeth
And his untimely frenzy thus awaketh :
' Dear Lord, thy sorrow to my sorrow lendeth
Another power ; no flood by raining slaketh.
My woe too sensible thy passion maketh
  More feeling-painful : let it then suffice
  To drown one woe, one pair of weeping eyes. 1680

' And for my sake, when I might charm thee so,
For she that was thy Lucrece, now attend me :
Be suddenly revenged on my foe,
Thine, mine, his own : suppose thou dost defend me
From what is past : the help that thou shalt lend me
  Comes all too late, yet let the traitor die,
  For sparing justice feeds iniquity.

' But ere I name him, you fair lords,' quoth she,
(Speaking to those that came with Collatine)
' Shall plight your honourable faiths to me, 1690
With swift pursuit to venge this wrong of mine,
For 'tis a meritorious fair design
  To chase injustice with revengeful arms :
  Knights, by their oaths, should right poor ladies' harms.'

At this request, with noble disposition,
Each present lord began to promise aid,
As bound in knighthood to her imposition,
Longing to hear the hateful foe bewray'd.
But she, that yet her sad task hath not said,
    The protestation stops. ' O, speak,' quoth she,   1700
    ' How may this forced stain be wip'd from me ?

' What is the quality of my offence,
Being constrain'd with dreadful circumstance ?
May my pure mind with the foul act dispense,
My low-declined honour to advance ?
May any terms acquit me from this chance ?
    The poison'd fountain clears itself again ;
    And why not I from this compelled stain ? '

With this, they all at once began to say,
Her body's stain her mind untainted clears ;   1710
While with a joyless smile she turns away
The face, that map which deep impression bears
Of hard misfortune, carv'd in it with tears.
    ' No, no,' quoth she, ' no dame hereafter living
    By my excuse shall claim excuse's giving.'

Here with a sigh, as if her heart would break,
She throws forth Tarquin's name : ' He, he,' she says,
But more than ' he ' her poor tongue could not speak ;
Till after many accents and delays,
Untimely breathings, sick and short assays,   1720
    She utters this : ' He, he, fair lords, 'tis he,
      That guides this hand to give this wound to me.'

Even here she sheathed in her harmless breast
A harmful knife, that thence her soul unsheathed :
That blow did bail it from the deep unrest
Of that polluted prison where it breathed :
Her contrite sighs unto the clouds bequeathed
    Her winged sprite, and through her wounds doth fly
      Life's lasting date from cancell'd destiny.

Stone-still, astonish'd with this deadly deed,   1730
Stood Collatine, and all his lordly crew ;
Till Lucrece' father, that beholds her bleed,
Himself on her self-slaughter'd body threw,
And from the purple fountain Brutus drew
    The murderous knife, and, as it left the place,
      Her blood, in poor revenge, held it in chase ;

And bubbling from her breast, it doth divide
In two slow rivers, that the crimson blood
Circles her body in on every side,
Who, like a late-sack'd island, vastly stood   1740
Bare and unpeopled, in this fearful flood.
      Some of her blood still pure and red remain'd,
      And some look'd black, and that false Tarquin stain'd.

About the mourning and congealed face
Of that black blood a watery rigol goes,
Which seems to weep upon the tainted place:
And ever since, as pitying Lucrece' woes,
Corrupted blood some watery token shows;
      And blood untainted still doth red abide,
      Blushing at that which is so putrified.   1750

'Daughter, dear daughter,' old Lucretius cries,
'That life was mine which thou hast here deprived.
If in the child the father's image lies,
Where shall I live now Lucrece is unlived?
Thou wast not to this end from me derived.
      If children pre-decease progenitors,
      We are their offspring and they none of ours.

' Poor broken glass, I often did behold
In thy sweet semblance my old age new born,
But now that fair fresh mirror, dim and old,   1760
Shows me a bare-bon'd death by time outworn :
O, from thy cheeks my image thou hast torn,
    And shiver'd all the beauty of my glass,
    That I no more can see what once I was.

' O time, cease thou thy course and last no longer,
If they surcease to be that should survive.
Shall rotten death make conquest of the stronger,
And leave the faltering feeble souls alive ?
The old bees dies, the young possess their hive ;
    Then live, sweet Lucrece, live again, and see   1770
    Thy father die, and not thy father thee ! '

By this starts Collatine as from a dream,
And bids Lucretius give his sorrow place,
And then in key-cold Lucrece' bleeding stream
He falls, and bathes the pale fear in his face,
And counterfeits to die with her a space ;
    Till manly shame bids him possess his breath,
    And live to be revenged on her death.

157

The deep vexation of his inward soul
Hath serv'd a dumb arrest upon his tongue ; 1780
Who, mad that sorrow should his use control
Or keep him from heart-easing words so long,
Begins to talk ; but through his lips do throng
    Weak words, so thick come in his poor heart's aid
    That no man could distinguish what he said.

Yet sometime ' Tarquin ' was pronounced plain,
But through his teeth, as if the name he tore.
This windy tempest, till it blow up rain,
Held back his sorrow's tide, to make it more ;
At last it rains, and busy winds give o'er, 1790
    Then son and father weep with equal strife,
    Who should weep most for daughter or for wife.

The one doth call her his, the other his,
Yet neither may possess the claim they lay.
The father says ' She 's mine.' ' O, mine she is,'
Replies her husband : ' do not take away
My sorrow's interest, let no mourner say
    He weeps for her, for she was only mine,
    And only must be wail'd by Collatine.'

'O,' quoth Lucretius, 'I did give that life   1800
Which she too early and too late hath spill'd.'
'Woe, woe,' quoth Collatine, 'she was my wife,
I ow'd her, and 'tis mine that she hath kill'd.'
'My daughter' and 'my wife' with clamours fill'd
        The dispers'd air, who, holding Lucrece' life,
        Answer'd their cries, 'my daughter' and 'my wife.'

Brutus, who pluck'd the knife from Lucrece' side,
Seeing such emulation in their woe,
Began to clothe his wit in state and pride,
Burying in Lucrece' wound his folly's show.   1810
He with the Romans was esteemed so
        As silly jeering idiots are with kings,
        For sportive words and uttering foolish things:

But now he throws that shallow habit by
Wherein deep policy did him disguise,
And arm'd his long-hid wits advisedly
To check the tears in Collatinus' eyes.
'Thou wronged lord of Rome,' quoth he, 'arise:
        Let my unsounded self, suppos'd a fool,
        Now set thy long-experienc'd wit to school.   1820

' Why, Collatine, is woe the cure for woe ?
Do wounds help wounds, or grief help grievous deeds ?
Is it revenge to give thyself a blow
For his foul act, by whom thy fair wife bleeds ?
Such childish humour from weak minds proceeds :
  Thy wretched wife mistook the matter so,
  To slay herself, that should have slain her foe.

' Courageous Roman, do not steep thy heart
In such relenting dew of lamentations,
But kneel with me and help to bear thy part, 1830
To rouse our Roman gods with invocations
That they will suffer these abominations,
  (Since Rome herself in them doth stand disgraced)
  By our strong arms from forth her fair streets chased.

' Now, by the Capitol that we adore,
And by this chaste blood so unjustly stained,
By heaven's fair sun that breeds the fat earth's store,
By all our country rights in Rome maintained,
And by chaste Lucrece' soul that late complained
  Her wrongs to us, and by this bloody knife, 1840
  We will revenge the death of this true wife ! '

This said, he struck his hand upon his breast,
And kiss'd the fatal knife, to end his vow,
And to his protestation urg'd the rest,
Who, wondering at him, did his words allow:
Then jointly to the ground their knees they bow,
    And that deep vow, which Brutus made before,
    He doth again repeat, and that they swore.

When they had sworn to this advised doom,
They did conclude to bear dear Lucrece thence, 1850
To show her bleeding body thorough Rome,
And so to publish Tarquin's foul offence:
Which being done with speedy diligence,
    The Romans plausibly did give consent
    To Tarquin's everlasting banishment.

THE PHŒNIX AND TURTLE

THE PHŒNIX AND TURTLE

LET the bird of loudest lay,
On the sole Arabian tree,
Herald sad and trumpet be,
To whose sound chaste wings obey.

But thou shrieking harbinger,
Foul precurrer of the fiend,
Augur of the fever's end,
To this troop come thou not near !

From this session interdict
Every fowl of tyrant wing,   10
Save the eagle, feather'd king :
Keep the obsequy so strict.

Let the priest in surplice white,
That defunctive music can,
Be the death-divining swan,
Lest the requiem lack his right.

And thou treble-dated crow,
That thy sable gender mak'st
With the breath thou giv'st and tak'st,
'Mongst our mourners shalt thou go.　　　20

Here the anthem doth commence :
Love and constancy is dead,
Phœnix and the turtle fled,
In a mutual flame from hence.

So they loved, as love in twain
Had the essence but in one,
Two distincts, division none,
Number there in love was slain.

Hearts remote, yet not asunder ;
Distance and no space was seen　　　30
'Twixt the turtle and his queen :
But in them it were a wonder.

So between them love did shine,
That the turtle saw his right
Flaming in the phœnix' sight ;
Either was the other's mine.

Property was thus appalled,
That the self was not the same;
Single nature's double name
Neither two nor one was called.   40

Reason in itself confounded
Saw division grow together,
To themselves yet either neither,
Simple were so well compounded;

That it cried, How true a twain
Seemeth this concordant one!
Love hath reason, reason none,
If what parts can so remain.

Whereupon it made this threne,
To the phœnix and the dove,   50
Co-supremes and stars of love,
As chorus to their tragic scene.

THRENOS

Beauty, truth, and rarity,
Grace in all simplicity,
Here enclos'd in cinders lie.

Death is now the phœnix' nest,
And the turtle's loyal breast
To eternity doth rest,

Leaving no posterity :
'Twas not their infirmity,   60
It was married chastity.

Truth may seem, but cannot be,
Beauty brag, but 'tis not she,
Truth and beauty buried be.

To this urn let those repair
That are either true or fair ;
For these dead birds sigh a prayer.

Notes

VENUS AND ADONIS

158. *seize love upon thy left*; *i.e.* ' clasp your own left hand as a lover would.'

515. *slips*; one sense of *slips* is ' pieces of counterfeit money,' and there is probably a play on this.

599. *Tantalus*; Tantalus was punished in Hades by being placed in a pool of water, with a bough of delicious fruit over his head, and tormented with hunger and thirst: when he tried to drink, the water receded; when to eat, the bough rose out of his reach.

704. *indenting*; to indent is to cut along a wavy or zigzag line between the two similar halves of a document drawn in duplicate, so that the halves exactly tally. Hence it came to mean to follow a zigzag course.

1062. *Her eyes*; this must apparently mean that her eyes reproach themselves that they have previously wept on inadequate excuse.

1064. *three*; it is perhaps just worth comparing the three sums of 3 *Henry VI*, II. i. 25.

THE RAPE OF LUCRECE

8. *Hap'ly . . . unhapp'ly*; printed just as in Q 1 to point the play on words.

19. *such high proud rate*; Q 5 reads *so high a rate*.

24. *morning*; so Q 1 (Bod. 1). The rest *mornings*, which is easier in sense, if less good in sound.

26. *An expir'd date, cancell'd ere well begun*; Q 5 reads *A date expir'd; and cancell'd ere begun*.

52-70. The general sense is clear, and I doubt if it is worth while trying to explicate by paraphrase the intricate involutions of this elaborately 'conceited' passage. One point however may be mentioned. It is possible that the *ore* of Q 1 in l. 56 should be modernised not (as here and usually) into *o'er*, but into *or* (i.e. heraldic gold), and that we should follow Wyndham in taking the meaning to be 'stain the blushes *into* or with white,' since, as Wyndham points out, Guillim, in his *Display of Heraldrie*, explains that or is produced by joining two parts of white with one of red.

117. *mother*; Q 5 reads *sad source*, and two lines later reads *shuts* for *stows*.

125, 6. This is the reading of Q 1 (Bod. 1). The rest read *themselves betake* and *wake*.

135. *That what they have not . . .*; something is pretty clearly wrong here. Q 5 reads *That oft they have not that which they possess*, which seems possible enough till we get to l. 137, which determines, I think, the required sense, namely 'They scatter what they possess for what they have not.' The suggestions *For what* and *Of what* would in different ways both give this sense, though neither is graphically easy, though we can suppose that, *For what* having been first written, a *that* which was supposed to displace *what* in fact displaced *For*.

154. *Sinon*; by a false story persuaded the Trojans to receive the wooden horse, in which the Greek warriors were concealed, into the city.

245. *painted cloth*; the painted cloths, cheap substitutes for tapestry, had (as well as pictures) moral maxims on them.

268-71. Q 5, disliking the double rhyme, reads *pleads*, *dreads*, and *leads*.

352. *My will is back'd with resolution*; if this line stood alone we

should certainly read the last word as five syllables; but it is clear from ll. 354 and 355 that we are dealing with a double rhyme, and therefore that this line is a foot short.

531. *a pure compound*; Q 5 reads *purest compounds*.

542. *pure piety*; it is an interesting study in the perpetuation of errors to see how many editions, without either justification or comment, read *true piety*.

684. *prone*; Q 5 reads *foule*.

858. *Tantalus*; see note on *Venus and Adonis*, 599.

950. *cherish springs*; it is possible to extract sense by taking *springs* to mean young shoots as contrasted with the old oak, but the general run of the sense here concentrates attention so much on the destructive powers of Time that one sympathises with Warburton's and Johnson's uneasiness, the former wanting to read 'tarish' (French 'tarir, to dry up,') and the latter 'perish,' in an active sense.

1123. *mute and dumb*; Q 5 reads *ever dumb*.

1128, 1134. *Philomel*; was ravished by Tereus, and subsequently changed into a nightingale.

1155. *death reproach's debtor*; (Q 1 in fact reads *death reproches detter*). Malone took this to mean that death was a debt which she owed to the reproach of her conscience. But apart from the difficulty of extracting that meaning from the words, it is not surely the meaning that is wanted, since it would throw the weight of the argument in favour of death, whereas Lucrece goes on at once to say that death would merely add pollution of soul to that of body. The lines surely represent a real dilemma, so that we want the sense 'Life is shamed, so that it would be better to die, but death would also be shameful, so that it may be better to live.' But I confess that I do not see how to extract that meaning either from the lines, unless we suppose that death being reproach's debtor means no more than that death would be liable to reproach.

1544. *Tarquin armed to beguild*; so Q 1, and for the matter of that the six succeeding Qq, so that it does not appear that their compositors or press-correctors found it suspicious. Malone read *Tarquin armed; so beguil'd*, taking *beguil'd* in the sense of 'beguiling,' while Steevens, accepting the same reading, interpreted *beguil'd* as 'masked.' Wyndham raises various points against this emendation, one of which seems to me perfectly decisive, namely that though Tarquin no doubt was armed there is no sort of relevance in saying so here; *i.e.* he must be armed metaphorically, and probably for some purpose or other. Hence Knox Pooler's suggestion of *Tarquin, armed so, beguil'd* is a great deal more acceptable than Malone's, since the *armed so* means equipped like Sinon. But it still suffers from the disadvantage that in a carefully printed text the error of *to* for *so* is surprising. And I find Wyndham's positive suggestion much less convincing than his negative. He would read *begild*, pointing out quite rightly that *guild* for *gild* is found. But the rhyme is awkward, and so is the absolute use of *begild* without an object. Knox Pooler says that he once thought *beguild* might be a corrupt form of *beguile* (cf. *vilde* and *vile*), and if there were evidence for this it would solve the whole problem, since the one thing perfectly clear is that *beguile* would give precisely the sense wanted, and that the only objection to it is its failure to rhyme.

THE PHŒNIX AND TURTLE

This trifle, for trifle it is, is yet in its way so perfect, and has compressed in it so much more than a casual reading displays, that it perhaps deserves more comment that it sometimes receives.

The poem falls into four sections: (*a*) 1-20, an Introduction; (*b*) 21-40, the Anthem; (*c*) 41-52, the comments of Reason; and (*d*) the Threnos.

(*a*) is quite simple; the bird (unspecified) with the loudest song is to act as trumpeter to summon the ' good ' birds to the obsequies. The screech-owl is banned, as are all birds of prey except the royal eagle. The priest is to be the swan, and one of the mourners the crow. (*b*) is very far from simple, and what begins as an anthem turns into a semi-philosophical disquisition full of the language of the schools. Its theme is the unity-in-duality and duality-in-unity of love; in (*c*) Reason has to admit that something which is repugnant to reason is nevertheless so; and that therefore love is right and reason wrong; (*d*) is a simple and lovely lament.

2. *sole*; Lyly tells us that as there is but one Phœnix in the world, so there is but one tree in Arabia wherein she buildeth; and in *The Tempest*, III. iii. 23, we have *one tree, the Phœnix' throne*. But there is probably also the sense of ' deserted.'

15. *death-divining*; i.e. his own death.

17. *treble-dated*; there is here probably a confusion between *cornix* (crow) and *corvus* (raven), since Pliny says that Hesiod says that the crow lives nine times as long as a man, a stag four times as long as a crow, and a raven three times as long as a stag. And further, it is of the raven that we are told that it conceives and lays its eggs at the bill, so that the *sable gender* means its black young.

27. *distincts*, *divisions*; in the language of the schools 'distinction' implies a verbal, 'division' a real, difference.

28. *Number . . . slain*; i.e. two are seen not to be two but one, or if we like, a more startling way of putting it, 'two-ness' becomes inexplicably 'one-ness.'

32. *But in them . . .* ; this would be a miracle except in them.

36. *Either was the other's mine*; cf. Donne, 'we two, one another's best.'

37. *Property . . . same*; the point here becomes clearer when we realise that in Shakespearean idiom 'self' and 'same' are almost always identical. The phrase means, I think, that the sense of the proper use of language is outraged by the discovery that a synonym is not a synonym.

43, 44. No satisfactory explanation has been advanced of these lines, and the truth, I think, is that the sense has to be felt and not arrived at by analysis.

52. *chorus*; i.e. the speaker of the epilogue.

(For these notes I am much indebted to Professor J. A. Smith for allowing me to read an unpublished—though one may hope some day to be published—paper of his in which he treats the problems with great acumen and in most illuminating detail.)

Glossary

MANY words and phrases in Shakespeare require glossing, not because they are in themselves unfamiliar, but for the opposite reason, that Shakespeare uses in their Elizabethan and unfamiliar sense a large number of words which seem so familiar that there is no incentive to look for them in the glossary. It is hoped that a glossary arranged as below will make it easy to see at a glance what words and phrases in any particular scene require elucidation. A number of phrases are glossed by what seems to be, in their context, the modern equivalent rather than by lexicographical glosses on the words which compose them.

Venus and Adonis

Dedication EARE, reap

line

9 STAIN TO, superior to (*i.e.* making them appear blemished)

11 WITH HERSELF AT STRIFE, 'in competition with herself'

40 PROVE, try

53 MISS, misbehaviour

56 TIRES, ravens

71 RANK, in spate

86 DIVE-DAPPER, dabchick

90 WINKS, shuts eyes

100 JAR, conflict

121 WINK, close eyes

135 RHEUMATIC, catarrhal

150 GROSS, heavy

181 SPRIGHT, spirit

204 UNKIND, unnatural; *i.e.* not having borne a child

line

205 CONTEMN ME THIS, deny this to me

222 INTENDMENTS, intentions

236 BOTTOM, valley

237 BRAKES, bushes

260 JENNET, small Spanish horse

271 COMPASS'D, arched

277 TOLD, counted

303 BID A BASE, challenge to chase (in game of prisoners' base)

314 VAILS, drops

343 WISTLY, attentively

368 MORTAL ROUND, earthly ball

395 BENDING CREST, arching mane

443 STILLITORY, still

456 FLAWS, gusts

457 ADVISEDLY, knowing what it meant

471 WITTILY, cunningly

174

line
472 FAIR FALL, good luck to
508 DANGEROUS, infectious
520 TOLD, counted
590 LAWN, fine linen
597 PROVE, try
598 MANAGE, control (as a horse)
600 CLIP, embrace
617 TUSHES, tusks
618 MORTAL, deadly
619 BATTLE, array
633 EYNE, eyes
636 ROOT, tears, ' rootles '
649 JEALOUSY, apprehension
653 DISTEMPERING, disordering
674 UNCOUPLE, loose your hounds
677 FEARFUL, frightened
682 CRANKS, twists
683 MUSIT, gap in hedge
687 CONIES, rabbits
715 LEAVE, leave off
725 CLOUDY, moody
740 WOOD, mad
743 IMPOSTHUME, abscess
747 FAVOUR, appearance
767 FRETS, erodes
782 CLOSURE, enclosure
787 REPROVE, rebut
797 BEREAVES, destroys

line
808 TEEN, woe
813 LAWND, lawn
826 MISTRUSTFUL, not to be trusted
838 FOOLISH-WITTY, foolish-wise
850 HUMOUR OF FANTASTIC WITS,
whims of would-be clever
young men
854 CABINET, bedroom
870 COASTETH, hastens
874 STRICT, constricting
888 STRAIN COURTESY, make way for
each other (' after you ! ')
COPE, encounter
895 ECSTASY, dumbfounderment
907 SPLEENS, moods
909 MATED, made helpless (check-
mated)
921 WELKIN, sky
956 VAIL'D, lowered
995 CLEPES, entitles
996 SUPREME, *as noun*
1010 SUSPECT, suspicion
1012 INSINUATE, flatter
1018 MUTUAL, general
1094 FEAR, frighten
1105 URCHIN, hedgehog
1151 SILLY, simple

The Rape of Lucrece

line		line	
1	POST, haste	207	CIPHER, indicate
2	TRUSTLESS, untrustworthy		FONDLY, madly
9	BATELESS, unblunted	208	NOTE, brand of disgrace
10	LET, cease	214	TOY, trifle
14	PECULIAR, particular	216	FOND, foolish
32	SINGULAR, rare	221	SIEGE, attack
37	SUGGESTED, tempted	236	QUITTAL, requital
40	BRAVING COMPARE, challenging comparison	244	SAW, proverb
		258	LAWN, fine linen
47	LIVER, *seat of passion*	284	FOND, foolish
57	ENTITULED, blazoned	303	WARD, guard
93	PLEATS, folds of a robe	304	RATE, chide
100	PARLING, speaking	313	CONDUCT, guide
104	MORALIZE, interpret	324	CONSTERS, construes
112	GREETS, thanks	327	HOURLY DIAL, clock
116	WELKIN, sky	328	WHO, which (*sc.* 'bars' or perhaps 'dial')
134	FOND, foolish		
144	GAGE, risk		LET, hinder
151	DEFECT, lack	333	SNEAPED, pinched with cold
164	COMFORTABLE, comforting	335	SHELVES, ledges of rock
167	SILLY, innocent	373	BEREAVES, dazzles
169	LEAPT, *participle*	375	WINK, close
180	ADVISEDLY, deliberately	424	QUALIFIED, moderated
196	WEED, robe	429	OBDURATE, hardened
200	FANCY, love	443	GOVERNESS, *fem. of* governor
201	RESPECT, discrimination	458	WINKING, with eyes shut
202	DIGRESSION, transgression	459	ANTICS, grotesque shapes
205	COAT, coat-of-arms	471	HEARTLESS, frightened
206	DASH, one of the 'abatements of honour' of which the bar sinister was an example	472	PEERS, causes to peer
		476	COLOUR, excuse
		507	COUCHETH, causes to cower